The Constitution, Citizenship, and Immigration in American History, 1790—2000

Other Titles in this Series:

The War Power: Original and Contemporary
by **Louis Fisher**

Women and the U.S. Constitution, 1776–1920
by **Jean H. Baker**

The Rights Revolution in the Twentieth Century
by **Mark V. Tushnet**

Federalism across the Nineteenth Century: 1787–1905
by **James W. Ely Jr.**

Race and the Constitution: From the Philadelphia Convention to the Age of Segregation
by **Paul Finkelman**

Religion, Morality, and the Constitutional Order
by **Linda Przybyszewski**

To order these and other AHA publications, visit:
www.historians.org/AHAstore

The Constitution, Citizenship, and Immigration in American History, 1790–2000

by **Kunal M. Parker**

Published by the
American Historical Association
400 A Street, SE
Washington, D.C. 20003
www.historians.org

and sponsored by the
Institute for Constitutional History
at the New-York Historical Society
and the George Washington University Law School

KUNAL M. PARKER is a Professor of Law and Dean's Distinguished Scholar at the University of Miami School of Law. Please address all correspondence to kparker@law.miami.edu. He would like to thank David Abraham, Rebecca Sharpless, and the editors for their comments. Zachary Hammond helped with citations.

AHA EDITORS: Sarah Fenton, Liz Townsend

LAYOUT: Chris Hale

The New Essays on American Constitutional History series is also sponsored by the Institute for Constitutional History at the New-York Historical Society and the George Washington University Law School.

© 2013 by the American Historical Association
ISBN: 978-0-87229-199-7

All rights reserved. No part of this book may be reproduced in any form without permission in writing from the publisher, except by a reviewer who wishes to quote brief passages in connection with a review written for inclusion in a magazine or newspaper.

Published in 2013 by the American Historical Association. As publisher, the American Historical Association does not adopt official views on any field of history and does not necessarily agree or disagree with the views expressed in this book.

Library of Congress Cataloging-in-Publication Data:

Parker, Kunal Madhukar, 1968–

The constitution, citizenship, and immigration in American history, 1790–2000 / by Kunal M. Parker.

pages cm. —(New essays on American constitutional history series)

Includes bibliographical references and index.

ISBN 978-0-87229-199-7

1. Citizenship—United States—History. 2. Emigration and immigration law—United States—History. I. Title.

KF4700.P37 2013

342.7308'309--dc23   2012041803

Table of Contents

Series Introduction vii

Introduction 1

Towards Dred Scott: The Constitution, Immigration,
and Citizenship from the American Revolution
to the Civil War 9

The Era of Racial Restriction: Immigration, Citizenship,
and the Constitution from the Civil War
to the Mid-Twentieth Century 23

A Rights Revolution? Immigration and Citizenship
in the Post-World War II Period 35

Conclusion 51

Further Reading 53

Notes 57

Series Introduction

New Essays on American Constitutional History is published by the American Historical Association, in association with the Institute for Constitutional Studies. This series follows the lead of its predecessor, the Bicentennial Essays on the Constitution, published by the AHA under the editorship of Herman Belz as part of the commemoration of the two hundredth anniversary of the Constitution over two decades ago. The goal remains the same. The essays are intended to provide both students and teachers with brief, accessible, and reliable introductions to some of the most important aspects of American constitutional development. The essays reflect the leading scholarship in the field and address topics that are classic, timely, and always important.

American constitutionalism is characterized by a series of tensions. Such tensions are persistent features of American constitutional history, and they make a frequent appearance in these essays. The American tradition emphasizes the importance of written constitutions. The United States Constitution declares that "this Constitution" is the "supreme law of the land." But time moves on. Politics and society are ever changing. How do we manage the tension between being faithful to a written constitutional text and adapting to changing political circumstances? To the extent that the American brand of constitutionalism binds us to the past, creates stability, and slows political change, how do we balance these conservative forces with the pressures of the moment that might demand departures from inherited ways of doing things and old ideas about rights and values? We sometimes change the terms of the old text through amendment or wholesale replacement of one constitution with another (from the Articles of Confederation to the Constitution at the national level, or more often at the state level), but we apply and adapt the inherited constitutional text through interpretation and practice. All the while, we manage the tension between being faithful to the text that we have and embracing the "living constitution" that grows out of that text.

Law figures prominently in the American constitutional tradition. Our written constitutions are understood to be fundamental laws and part of our legal code. They are the foundation of our legal system and superior to all other laws. They provide legally enforceable rules for judges and others to follow. Judges and lawyers play an important role in interpreting American constitutions and translating the bare bones of the original text into the detailed body of doctrine known as constitutional law. It has often been the dream of judges, lawyers, and legal scholars to insulate constitutional law from the world of politics. There is a long-held aspiration for judges and lawyers to be able to spin out constitutional law in accord with established principles of justice, reason, and tradition. But politics has also been central to the history of American constitutionalism. Constitutions are created by political actors and serve political purposes. Once in place, constitutional rules and values are politically contested, and they are interpreted and put into practice by politicians and political activists, as well as by judges. The tension between law and politics is a persistent one in American constitutional history.

A final tension of note has been between power and liberty. In the modern tradition, constitutional government is limited government. Constitutions impose limits and create mechanisms for making those constraints effective. They specify what the boundaries of government power are and what rights individuals and groups have against government. But there is also an older tradition, in which constitutions organize and empower government. The U.S. Constitution contains both elements. Many of its provisions, especially the amendments, limit government. These are some of the most celebrated features of the Constitution, and they have become the basis for much of the constitutional law that has been developed by the judiciary. But the Constitution was specifically adopted to empower the federal government and create new, better institutions that could accomplish national objectives. Both the U.S. Constitution and the state constitutions are designed to gather and direct government power to advance the public good. Throughout American constitutional history, judges, politicians, and activists have struggled over the proper balance between empowering government and limiting government and over the best understanding of the rights of individuals and the public welfare.

These essays examine American constitutionalism, not a particular constitutional text. The U.S. Constitution figures prominently in these essays, as it does in American history, but the American constitutional tradition includes other foundational documents, including notably the state constitutions. These texts are a guide to the subject matter of these essays, but they are not exhaustive of it. Laws, court decisions, administrative actions, and custom, along with founding documents, perform constitutional functions in the American political system, just as they do in the British system where there is no single written "constitution." Whether "written" or "unwritten," constitutions perform certain common tasks. Constitutions define the organic structures of government, specifying the basic institutions for making and implementing public policy, including the processes for altering the constitution itself. Constitutions distribute powers among those institutions of government, delegating, enumerating, prohibiting, and reserving powers to each governmental body. The flip side of entrusting power and discretion to governmental bodies is the definition of limits on those powers, the specification of individual and collective rights. Constitutions also specify who participates in the institutions of government and how and to whom the power of government applies. That is, constitutions identify the structures of citizenship and political jurisdiction. Across its seven articles and twenty-seven amendments, the U.S. Constitution addresses all of these topics, but the text is only a starting point. These topics form the subject matter of New Essays on American Constitutional History.

Writing early in the twentieth century, the great constitutional historian Edward Corwin observed that relatively few citizens actually read the U.S. Constitution, despite its brevity. He thought that this was in part because the "real constitution of the United States has come to mean something very different from the document" itself. The document laid out the framework of government, but "the real scope of the powers which it should exercise and of the rights which it should guarantee was left, to a very great extent, for future developments to determine." Understanding American constitutionalism requires understanding American constitutional history. It is a history of contestation and change, creation and elaboration. These essays aim to illuminate that history.

—*Keith E. Whittington,*
Princeton University

—*Gerry Leonard,*
Boston University School of Law

Introduction

Over the centuries, prominent Americans have joined their country's self-image as a nation of immigrants to its self-image as a universal nation founded on abstract values. In the late eighteenth century, as Americans were beginning their struggle to break with Great Britain, Thomas Paine triumphantly declared his adopted country "an asylum for mankind"—a refuge for the entire human species, a beacon for oppressed peoples everywhere.[1] In the mid-nineteenth century, in the years of mass migration from northwestern Europe, Herman Melville made the link in even more grandiose terms, claiming that "American blood" stood for "the blood of the whole world" and that Americans were "the heirs of all time."[2] In the late nineteenth and early twentieth centuries, as the country experienced even greater migration from all over Europe, as well as from Asia and the Americas, thinkers once again underscored the link between immigration and universalism. Emma Lazarus's widely celebrated poem "The New Colossus," written in 1883 to celebrate the Statue of Liberty, announced a "world-wide welcome" for "huddled masses yearning to breathe free."[3] Israel Zangwill's early twentieth-century drama *The Melting Pot* hailed America's ability to absorb immigrants effortlessly from many different nations even as the play's title secured a permanent place in the everyday American lexicon.[4] In the wake of the Second World War and in the context of renewed discussions over immigration, presidential hopeful John F. Kennedy's *A Nation of Immigrants* once again joined immigration and universal values as part of the logic of American history.[5]

The powerful strand of thought linking immigration and universalism as the very ontology of America appears to find confirmation in brute numbers. From the early nineteenth to the early twentieth century, the United States attracted three-fifths of all the world's immigrants, more than those received by all other large immigrant-receiving countries in the world combined.[6] It remained the world's largest immigrant-receiving country throughout the twentieth century. In the early decades of the twenty-first century, it has continued to admit over a million immigrants annually to permanent residence.[7] Furthermore, throughout its history as an independent nation, the United States has adopted liberal naturalization policies relative to those of most other countries, thereby facilitating immigrants' quick incorporation into the polity.[8]

Despite this unquestionably impressive record of receiving and absorbing immigrants, the reality of American immigration policy has fallen far short of the rhetoric celebrating openness and universalism. If the United States has celebrated itself noisily as a universal nation of immigrants, it has never welcomed all possible entrants. For example, in the mid-nineteenth century, even as Herman Melville was equating "American blood" with "the blood of the whole world," Justice Grier of the U.S. Supreme Court, adopting what was then a *pro*-immigration judicial stance, described America's immigration policy rather more restrictively: "It is the cherished policy of the general government to encourage and invite Christian foreigners of our own race to seek an asylum within our borders, and to convert these waste lands into productive farms, and thus add to the wealth, population, and power of the nation."[9] And even Grier's characterization of American immigration policy—open and welcoming as he undoubtedly thought it, and controversial as many at the time might have found it—might have been too broad. It was never the case even that all "Christian foreigners of our own race" could immigrate to the United States without legal impediment.

Over the centuries, as instantiated in an increasingly restrictive immigration law, different images of the desirable immigrant have appeared and receded, reflecting changes in the country's political, social, economic, and cultural make-up. Some of the distinguishing traits of the desirable immigrant over the course of two centuries of American history might be listed as follows: white, healthy, heterosexual, male, Protestant, sturdy republican farmer, unskilled worker, agricultural laborer, refugee from Communism, highly skilled worker, high net worth investor. Correspondingly, the undesirable, the excludable, and the removable have variously included the indigent, the criminal, the sick and disabled, the illiterate, polygamists, prostitutes, homosexuals, the undocumented, Anarchists, Communists, nonwhites (with a particular focus on Asians), and, more recently, terrorists. Furthermore, from the country's inception until the early 1950s—in short, for approximately three-quarters of its history as an independent nation—race has barred various groups either from being considered citizens at birth or from naturalizing. Membership in a Communist party could also serve as an obstacle to citizenship.

An essay on the historical relationship of the U.S. Constitution to questions of immigration and citizenship must come to terms with how the document has applied to the shifting realities of the state's dealings with immigrants. At the outset, it is safe to say that the Constitution, as interpreted by the U.S. Supreme Court, has never come in the way of the basic right of government to exclude and remove noncitizens from its territory. Drawing upon international law theory, the Court has repeatedly maintained that territorial sovereigns possess the right to defend a territorial inside from a territorial outside, even as they possess the right to protect the community of citizens from the presence of undesirable noncitizens. In *New York v. Miln* (1837), the Court approvingly quoted the eighteenth-century Swiss international law theorist Emmerich de Vattel, whom it characterized as "a standard writer upon public law," for the following proposition: "The sovereign may forbid the entrance of his territory either to foreigners in general, or in particular cases, to certain persons, or for certain particular purposes, according as he may think it advantageous to the state."[10]

This basic legal principle has remained unshaken, but has raised many different questions yielding varied answers over the long sweep of American history. Which sovereign—the federal or the state government—possesses the basic right to legislate in matters of immigration and citizenship? Which is the relevant community of citizens that might be defended against the presence of noncitizens, the national community or the state community? Who is a member of the relevant community of citizens that might be defended from the incursions of outsiders? Who might therefore be kept out of, or removed from, this community of citizens? Given that government possesses the basic right to exclude and remove noncitizens from its territory and polity, how, if at all, is that right limited by the Constitution? To what extent has the Constitution protected—or failed to protect—immigrants? This essay sorts such questions into three chronological sections: from the American Revolution to the Civil War; from the Civil War to World War II; and from World War II to the present.

From the American Revolution until the Civil War, the legal distinction between insider and outsider, citizen and noncitizen, could not easily be organized around whether an individual had or had not been born within American territory. Native Americans were not considered U.S. or state citizens despite having been born within territories the United States and the individual states claimed as their own. Neither were native-born blacks citizens of the national and (many) state polities. Northern and southern states could, and did, exclude and remove native-born free blacks from their territories. In some cases, slave states even assimilated native-born free blacks from other states to the legal status of aliens. None of this, as the Court's decision in *Dred Scott v. Sandford* (1857) confirmed, was constitutionally problematic.[11] Furthermore, being a U.S. or state citizen did not guarantee rights to move freely throughout the country. Such rights were withheld regardless of race from the native-born poor, who might be barred from moving from state to state, or even within states. All of this had profound consequences for immigrants. The disabilities visited upon immigrants—barriers to territorial entry and residence as well as exclusions from the polity—were disabilities that immigrants shared with large segments of the native-born population. Antebellum America was a country of external foreigners (immigrants from foreign countries) and internal foreigners (those born within national territory).

This variegated legal landscape was part of a world in which the states were far more powerful vis-à-vis the federal government than they would be after 1865. The Constitution did not—and still does not—explicitly vest an immigration power in the federal government. When questions about the locus of authority to regulate immigration came up, as they did increasingly after 1820, the constitutional debate was typically organized around whether the federal government possessed the authority to regulate immigration under the aegis of the Constitution's Commerce Clause or whether the states, who had been regulating immigrant traffic since colonial times, possessed the right to regulate the influx of outsiders pursuant to their police powers, the basic sovereign right to legislate for the health, welfare, and safety of the population. Throughout the antebellum period, even as the Court's developing Commerce Clause jurisprudence pointed towards recognizing a federal immigration power, the slave states' insistence on regulating free blacks' access to their territories brought about a countervailing emphasis on the importance of state police power to regulate outsiders' access to territory. Thus, slavery, native-born blacks' lack of national and state citizenship, and the slave states' paranoia surrounding the ingress of free blacks—in short, the status of blacks as internal foreigners—kept immigration authority in the hands of states, albeit suspended in constitutional flux, until the Civil War.

The Civil War and the passage of the Fourteenth Amendment marked the death knell of state-level immigration regimes that had regulated immigration since the late eighteenth century. Not until the Fourteenth Amendment extended citizenship to the entire native-born population did it become possible for a full-fledged federal immigration state (this use of "state" refers to the state that regulates immigration), replete with its own bureaucracy, to emerge. Only when the formal internal "foreignnesses" and borders of the antebellum years had been extinguished could a federal immigration state focused on external borders come into being.

In the post-Civil War decades, a period of massive immigration, the Court invented what has come to be known as the "plenary power doctrine." Even as it concentrated power over immigration and naturalization in the hands of the federal government, something that had not been possible in the antebellum period, the plenary power doctrine immunized the federal government's actions in these contexts from substantive constitutional review. Various provisions of the Constitution—from explicit procedural guarantees to prohibitions against *ex post facto* laws—were deemed inapplicable or unavailable to immigrants in the name of plenary federal power over immigration and naturalization.

Under the aegis of the plenary power doctrine, the federal government enacted a spate of legislation, introducing grounds of exclusion and deportation based on race, economics, morals, and political opinion, culminating in the wake of the First World War with explicit, racially motivated blanket bans on Asian immigration, and severe restrictions of southern and eastern European immigration. In keeping with its sanctioning of official racism in *Plessy v. Ferguson* (1896), but more importantly in the name of plenary power, the Court upheld racist and patriarchal federal immigration and citizenship laws and sanctioned state-level discrimination against immigrants.[12] But the very severity of the plenary power doctrine brought about some limitations on the doctrine stemming from the universalist language of the Fourteenth Amendment and from the invigoration of certain legal distinctions (procedure versus substance, presence within or outside territory, and so on) that occasionally redounded to the benefit of immigrants.

After World War II, the Court breathed new life into the Constitution's Due Process and Equal Protection clauses, setting up potent barriers to the kinds of racial and gender discrimination that had characterized so much of the country's history. At the constitutional level, however, at least when it came to the actions of the federal government in the context of immigration and naturalization, plenary power remained vital. Indeed, at the height of the Cold War, the Court's articulations of the plenary power doctrine were almost harsher than they had been in the late nineteenth century. However, as matter of federal statutory law, racial barriers to citizenship were lifted in the early 1950s and racist national origins quotas ended in 1965. Immigration and naturalization statutes reflected, in other words, the liberalization of the civil rights era. Immigration and naturalization law thus changed profoundly.

This is not to say that, especially in more recent years, the constitutional law of immigration and citizenship has not kept pace with more liberal statutory trends. When it comes to the activities of the federal government, however, the Court has engineered change in a muted, oblique, or osmotic way consistent with its earlier efforts to soften the harshness of the plenary power doctrine through judicial manipulations of porous legal distinctions (substance versus procedure, presence or absence from territory, degree of connection to the United States, and so on). Occasional glimmerings— buried in footnotes and stray observations—suggest that substantive provisions of the Constitution might be brought to bear on aspects of federal plenary power over immigration and citizenship. Nevertheless, the plenary power doctrine stands. Relative to state laws discriminating among citizens and aliens, by contrast, the Court has been much more aggressive than it was in the early twentieth century.

Looking back over the long span of the constitutional law of immigration and citizenship, several axes along which to organize the story suggest themselves: the shift from state to federal authority, with its attendant ambiguities and tensions; the Court's switch from analyzing immigration in terms of the Commerce Clause to analyzing it in terms of plenary power; the various constitutional limitations that have been slowly and confusedly brought to bear on federal and state power relating to immigrants; the increasing and then declining formal significance of race and national origins; and so on. While it touches on all of these, this essay emphasizes something else that runs through them all: the role of law in the production (and undermining) of the changing distinctions between "insider" and "outsider."

We tend to think of immigration as the movement of outsiders from other countries to our own. These outsiders are imagined to be noncitizens or aliens, just as those already in the country are imagined to be insiders and citizens. Until such time as immigrants become citizens, the various legal disabilities attaching to them (barriers to entry, vulnerability to removal, exclusion from various political, social, or economic benefits) are all imagined as incidents of, or stemming from, the basic fact that they come from somewhere else. This is how many people think of immigration. The foreign faces and accents, the long lines at consulates and at ports of entry, the news reports of undocumented immigrants attempting harrowing journeys across arid deserts and stormy seas all seem to confirm this.

But the historical record traced in this essay challenges this basic intuition. It shows not only how the law in general—and constitutional law in particular—has played a critical role in producing the foreignness of immigrants, but also how foreignness has been imbued with different meanings over time. This malleability of foreignness might allow one to question current arrangements and to imagine and bring into being different ones.

To begin with, American history reveals that birth within territory, or lack thereof, does not automatically mean one is an insider or citizen or an outsider or noncitizen. In the United States before 1865, birth within territory—if one happened to be Native American, black, or indigent— might not spare one from the legal disabilities we think of today as attaching uniquely to immigrants. One could be, in effect, a species of native-born alien. The Court and the Constitution played a critical role in bringing this state of affairs into being.

Even once birth within territory became a critical marker of who was or was not a citizen—as has been the case in the United States since 1865—there was no particular shape or form the disabilities associated with alienage had to take. Should government be vested with unfettered power when it came to dealing with immigrants or should it be hemmed in by constitutional precepts? Should government be allowed to produce strong substantive distinctions between citizens and aliens, on the one hand, or should such distinctions be weakened by regarding aliens as the beneficiaries of constitutional protections? Beginning in the late nineteenth century, by articulating the plenary power doctrine, the Court signaled to the federal government that it would possess virtually unfettered power over the exclusion, deportation, and naturalization of immigrants. At the same time, under the aegis of its alienage jurisprudence, the Court allowed state governments to discriminate among aliens and citizens in a range of contexts. It allowed, therefore, the production of a strong substantive distinction between citizen and alien, insider and outsider.

However, allowing government to draw strong substantive distinctions between citizens and aliens, insiders and outsiders, gave rise to difficulties for at least two reasons: first, outsiders could shade into insiders as result of territorial presence, extended residence within the community, and so on; second, governmental actions with respect to outsiders—for example, blanket bans on immigration from particular countries—inevitably affected insiders as well. To be sure, the Constitution provided no clear way to tell when outsiders became insiders, or when actions affecting outsiders affected insiders in constitutionally problematic ways. Here, too, there was room for play. Even as plenary power and its affiliated doctrines sanctioned the creation of strong substantive distinctions between insiders and outsiders, and hence the creation of fresh internal foreignness as the harsh treatment of outsiders had spillover effects on insiders, the Court sought to undermine strong governmental discriminations between insiders and outsiders. These ways of weakening governmental discriminations between insiders and outsiders have taken various forms over time: an insistence that certain provisions of the Constitution apply to all territorially present "persons"; an aggressive wielding of the Equal Protection and Due Process clauses against the states and, to a far lesser extent, the federal government; an invocation of distinctions between procedure and substance; and an insistence on procedural protections for immigrants.

The constitutional law of immigration and citizenship thus reveals two tendencies at odds with one another: on the one hand, that government might constitutionally draw sharp distinctions between citizen and alien, insider and outsider; on the other hand, that the status differences between citizen and alien be reduced in various ways. The tilt, it is fair to say, has always been in the direction of governmental power over immigrants, but the contours of these two tendencies, and the ways they have interacted over time, have proved far from predictable. This absence of predictability—combined with the historical malleability of birth within territory as a ground of membership—underscores the profound changeability of the lines that separate citizen from alien, insider from outsider. Such lines remain fluid, subject to change over the course of immigrants' struggles with the government.

Polyvalent terms such as "citizenship" and "immigration" may require more precise definitions. For the most part, this essay is concerned with "citizenship" in the sense of the formal legal distinction between "citizen" and "alien." Proceeding with such an understanding of citizenship, immigration law refers to the legal regime distinguishing between citizen and alien with respect to the terms on which the latter might enter, and remain within, the territory that the polity deems its own. In other words, immigration law polices the boundary between a territorial inside and a territorial outside on the basis of citizenship.

Working with such an understanding of citizenship and immigration does not mean, however, that it is ever possible or desirable to set aside another meaning of citizenship, that which concerns the quality and substance of internal membership in the polity, or what T. H. Marshall characterized as a historical agglomeration of civil, political, and social rights.[13] The distinction between citizenship in the sense of the formal legal distinction between citizen and alien, with which Marshall was unconcerned, and citizenship in the sense of internal membership in the polity, with which Marshall was concerned, might be illustrated through the example of native-born white women throughout the nineteenth century and into the early twentieth. Native-born white women were undeniably citizens of the United States in the sense that they were not aliens, but they were far from being full internal members of the polity by reason of being subjected to common law institutions such as coverture and being denied political rights.

Because the ways a state treats certain categories of alien cannot be separated from the ways in which it treats certain categories of the native-born, the history of citizenship as internal membership bleeds into the history of citizenship and immigration, particularly when it comes to disadvantaged members of society (women, racial minorities, and the indigent).[14] The treatment of outsiders is invariably a reflection of the treatment of insiders. For example, denying women the right to vote (along with other indicia of political membership) could not but feed, and be fed by, the view that a woman's citizenship was derivative of her husband's, and susceptible to forfeiture if she married an alien. Congress wrote this principle into the law of expatriation in the early twentieth century and the Court upheld it.

Towards Dred Scott:
The Constitution, Immigration, and Citizenship from the American Revolution to the Civil War

During the Confederation period, as individual states rushed to define their own citizenries and establish naturalization policies, there was also an emerging sense that the American Revolution had given rise to a single politico-legal and territorial community transcending state boundaries. This is reflected in the "comity clause" of Article IV of the Articles of Confederation:

> The better to secure and perpetuate mutual friendship and intercourse among the people of the different States in this Union, the free inhabitants of each of these States, paupers, vagabonds, and fugitives from justice excepted, shall be entitled to all privileges and immunities of free citizens in the several States; and the people of each state shall have free ingress and regress to and from any other State ... .[15]

By imposing the duty of comity on the individual states, this clause attempted to create something akin to a relationship between national membership and national territory. However, as James Madison pointed out at the time, the clause did so in a confused way by asking states to accord the "privileges and immunities of free *citizens*" to the "free *inhabitants*" of other states. The former referred to membership in the polity, the latter only to rights of legal residence.[16] One could, conceivably, possess an inhabitancy without being a citizen. Most revealing about the clause is the classes of individuals that it identified as *not* being the beneficiaries of this obligation of comity—namely, slaves, paupers, vagabonds, and fugitives from justice. When it came to these segments of the native-born population, the duty of comity disappeared: state borders could be thrown up as barriers to residence and movement.

With the formation of the United States at the end of the 1780s, the category of national citizenship emerged for the first time as the legal category that would define membership in the new national political community. An important feature of the new category of citizenship was that it was supposed to be the product of voluntary, as distinguished from involuntary and perpetual, allegiance. This idea of voluntary allegiance was consistent with the broader idea that the relationship between the political subject and the state was to be grounded in volition and consent. The English theory of *jus soli* subjecthood—widely seen in the late eighteenth century as a hallmark of monarchy and feudalism—held that subjects owed lifelong allegiance to the monarch by virtue of birth within the realm. Not surprisingly, in forging their break from Great Britain, Americans were quick to repudiate such a theory. The notion that allegiance could be chosen—and hence cast off—was important in justifying Americans' break from Great Britain. The two theories clashed in the impressment controversies of the late eighteenth century, with Great Britain's refusal to recognize sailors' right to abandon British subjecthood and the United States' insistence on their right to do so.[17]

As it turned out, the idea of voluntary citizenship, seductive as it appeared, was beset with contradictions from the outset. It should never be forgotten that Americans were able to claim voluntary citizenship as a hallmark of the nation in no small part because of coercion. The new regime of which voluntary citizenship was such an important part was a source of profound concern to a substantial portion of the resident population of the colonies who had no desire to give up their ties to their monarch. In large part, this population was coerced or intimidated into leaving the country (although many, principally slaves, were also coerced into accompanying those who left). As the historian Maya Jasanoff has written: "Confronting real doubts about their lives, liberty, and potential happiness in the United States, sixty thousand loyalists decided to follow the British and take their chances elsewhere in the British Empire. They took fifteen thousand black slaves with them—or about one in forty members of the American population."[18]

Furthermore, quite apart from its birth in war and coercion, voluntary citizenship itself was extended among the resident population by fiat. Those who remained after the loyalist exodus were not actually consulted or asked to choose. The idea of voluntary citizenship best applied, furthermore, to free white men. Legal dependents, a vast segment of the population including women, children, and slaves, were deemed incapable of exercising volition and hence of switching allegiance meaningfully. Under the common law institution of coverture, for example, the legal personhood of women was subsumed—in legal terminology, "covered"—by that of their husbands. This had consequences for women's ability to choose citizenship. A free married white woman who left the country in the company of her loyalist husband was not viewed as having exercised volition in choosing British subjecthood over American citizenship: she had simply, as was her duty, followed her husband. This worked in her favor because it might spare her the penalties inflicted upon male loyalists. As Theodore Sedgwick of the Massachusetts Supreme Judicial Court put it in the 1801 case of *Martin v. Massachusetts*, "A *wife* who left the country in the company of her husband did not *withdraw* herself; but was, if I may so express it, withdrawn by him. She did not deprive the government of the benefit of her personal services; she had none to render ... ."[19]

Even greater contradictions lay in the regime of citizenship applicable to future generations. Even as Americans cast off British subjecthood, the United States retained the basic *jus soli* or birthright subjecthood orientation of English law that was tainted in the Age of Revolution by its associations with feudalism and monarchy. In other words, citizenship would be conferred on those born within the territory of the United States. However, the *jus soli* principle was not spelled out in the Constitution. It probably worked best for native-born whites. At its inception, the Constitution did not deal with the question of whether those belonging to marginalized groups—free blacks, slaves, and Native Americans—qualified as U.S. citizens by reason of birth in U.S. territory. Subsequent developments would confirm that such groups did *not* count as U.S. citizens.

Despite the absence of any mention of *jus soli*, the Constitution did specify citizenship as a prerequisite to holding certain political offices.[20] It also made explicit the rules inducting aliens into the political community. Article I, Section 8, gave Congress the power to promulgate "a uniform rule of naturalization." In 1790, the first federal naturalization act limited naturalization to a "free white person" who had resided for two years in the United States, proved his "good character," and taken an oath "to support the constitution of the United States."[21] Only free white persons, in other words, could be inducted into the political community. The naturalization period was increased to five years by the Naturalization Act of 1795, and has remained at five years ever since, with a brief aberration in the late 1790s.[22]

Despite the emergence of the category of U.S. citizenship, membership in state polities remained important—most likely far more important— for everyday purposes than U.S. citizenship. The Constitution revamped the comity clause of the Articles of Confederation. Article IV, Section 1, provided that "the Citizens of each State shall be entitled to all Privileges and Immunities of Citizens in the several States." The embarrassing (and revealing) reference to "paupers, vagabonds and fugitives from justice" in the comity clause of the Articles of Confederation was removed. But the reference to *state* citizenship entitling an individual to "all Privileges and Immunities of Citizens in the several States" suggests that U.S. citizenship, at the country's inception, remained a relatively impoverished category.

The world of late eighteenth-century American citizenship might be described as follows. Of those born outside the country, only free whites could become U.S. citizens. When it came to the native-born population, certain segments—the ideal-typical propertied white males—were national and state citizens capable of enjoying and exercising the fullest panoply of available rights; others—white women and property-less white men—might not enjoy political rights at the national or state level but were clearly national citizens in terms of the citizen-alien distinction; and large segments of the population—blacks and Native Americans—were not even national citizens in terms of the citizen-alien distinction (although free blacks might be incorporated as members of the polities of some northern states). Were blacks and Native Americans suspended somewhere between citizen and alien? Were they aliens? An additional complication in this regard, unresolved until the Civil War, was the relationship between national and state citizenship. How did inclusions at the state level (for example, the incorporation of free blacks into the polities of certain states) relate to exclusions at the national level? Answers to such questions would be honed over the coming decades.

Although Congress acquired the constitutional authority to frame naturalization laws, it did not acquire the explicit constitutional authority to formulate a national immigration law. Neither did it attempt to establish one in practice. Indeed, at the national level, the concern with aliens lay not with their influx into, or presence within, territory, but with the alleged dangers of their participation in the political arena and the fear that they might subvert the young Republic. Segments of the American national leadership repeatedly expressed concerns about the capacity of aliens reared under monarchies or carried away by the excesses of the French Revolution to exercise republican citizenship in a responsible fashion. Evidence of these fears may be observed in the Constitutional Convention's debates over the qualifications for national political office and later, and more egregiously, in the Federalist anti-alien paranoia reflected in the passage of the Alien and Sedition Acts in the late 1790s, The point, however, is that immigration laws—those quotidian laws that determined outsiders' access to, and presence within, territory—remained in the hands of the states.

For the most part, in the decades immediately following the American Revolution, the states continued colonial policies for regulating access to their territories. Especially noteworthy about colonial restrictions is the seemingly indiscriminate way in which they mingled the dislike of territorial insiders and outsiders. The regulation of what was frequently labeled a "trade in persons"—i.e., the transport of indentured servants and redemptioners—appears to have been little more than an external manifestation of a well-developed internal regime for regulating natives' access to territory. The governing logic of this comprehensive system of territorial restriction can be found in American versions of the seventeenth-century English poor laws. The poor were to be denied territorial mobility *as the poor*, because of the fear that they would impose costs upon the places they entered, whether they entered such places from a place "beyond sea" or from a place just a few miles down the road. There was, then, no general legal right to free movement within the territory of one's birth. Natives and non-natives, insiders and outsiders, were disabled in similar ways.

Although states remained faithful to colonial poor relief models in many essentials, in the postindependence period they also began incrementally and confusedly to insert new categories of citizenship—federal *and* state—into these models. For example, under New York's 1788 Act for the Better Settlement and Relief of the Poor, shipmasters were required to report the names and occupations of all "persons" brought into the port of New York, and would be fined £20 for each unreported person, and £30 if such person was a "foreigner." The law further denied admission to "any person" who could not give a good account of himself to local authorities or was likely to become a charge to the city; such persons were to be returned "to the place whence he or she came."[23] Massachusetts chose to refer to state citizenship, rather than U.S. citizenship, in its legislation. Thus, in the early 1790s, in a dramatic departure from colonial practice, Massachusetts made citizenship "of this or any of the United States" (but, tellingly, not the brand new category of U.S. citizenship) a prerequisite to the acquisition of "settlement" or "inhabitancy" in a town, thereby making it impossible for noncitizens to acquire legal rights to residence and poor relief in the town where they lived, worked, and paid taxes. However, the same law also contained various provisions intended to make it difficult for citizens from other states, and Massachusetts citizens from other towns, to acquire legal residence.[24] Furthermore, the disabilities imposed upon natives and aliens—removal to the place of origin—remained comparable. Indeed, it was more likely for natives than for aliens to be removed, because the costs of transportation for the former were often lower.

This highly local understanding of the distinction between insider and outsider points to a central feature of systems of territorial restriction in the late eighteenth and early nineteenth centuries, namely that, even as territorial restrictions were promulgated at the state level, and began to incorporate the new categories of U.S. and state citizenship, individual cities and towns—rather than central state authorities, to say nothing of federal—were responsible in the first instance for the administration of poor relief and territorial restrictions. For the first several decades of its life as an independent nation, the United States' federal government and the Court remained largely uninvolved with immigration issues. But by the 1830s, the Court's judgment was increasingly solicited.

From the perspective of the constitutional law of immigration and citizenship, the period from 1830 to 1860 was one of flux. Mass immigration from Europe, depressed as a result of the Napoleonic wars, picked up after 1820, peaking during the Irish famine at mid-century. Yet immigration power remained at the state level, operating through relatively weak, inefficient, uncoordinated, and fractured bureaucracies. It would remain that way until after the Civil War.

The reasons for this are many, and surely include Jacksonian suspicions of overweening federal authority and defense of the traditional powers of states. But an even more important and specific reason was the insistence of the slave states on controlling outsiders' access to their territories so as to be able to exclude and remove free blacks, whether they had come from other states or other countries. The slave states' fear was that centralizing the power to regulate access to territory would deny them the authority to control the presence of free blacks, which would in turn damage slavery irreparably. To appease the slave states, internal borders had to remain in place, which left the defense of the external border chopped up, distributed among several different state authorities.

All of this made sense only because antebellum America remained a society in which substantial portions of the native-born population were not citizens, not just in the sense that they lacked the fullest panoply of available rights, but also in the legal sense of the distinction between citizen and alien. The entire native-born population also lacked unimpeded rights of residence and movement throughout national territory. I shall discuss this uneven distribution of citizenship and territorial rights before moving on to its implications for the constitutional law of immigration.

The disjunctures among citizenship, the native-born population, and rights of residence and movement lay at the heart of Native Americans' tragic history in the antebellum United States. After the Treaty of Paris in 1783, the United States claimed all lands east of the Mississippi ceded by Great Britain. After the ratification of the U.S. Constitution, the power to deal with Native Americans was fixed in the federal government. Article I, Section 8, of the Constitution gave Congress the power "to regulate Commerce with foreign Nations, and among the several States, and with the Indian Tribes."[25] This listing of Indian tribes along with foreign nations and domestic states reveals much about their awkward suspension between the domestic and the foreign, citizen and alien, outside the polity but inside its territory. Native Americans tribes were forced to sign treaties with the federal government.

In the 1830s, the Court endorsed the view that Native Americans were suspended between the status of citizen and alien. *Cherokee Nation v. Georgia* (1831), one of the Marshall Court's celebrated "Indian cases," adjudicated a dispute between the Cherokee tribe and the state of Georgia. When a Cherokee was captured by Georgia in Cherokee territory, and executed, the tribe argued that Georgia's acts violated various treaties between the Cherokees and the United States. In order for the Court to have jurisdiction over the case, it had to determine whether the Cherokees constituted a foreign state. According to the Court, the Cherokees were not inside the polity: they were not citizens in any sense. The many treaties with the Indian tribes "recognize[d] them as a people capable of maintaining the relations of peace and war" and hence as foreigners or aliens. At the same time, the Cherokees were also not aliens in any normal sense. They were different from other foreign sovereigns: "[t]he condition of the Indians in relation to the United States is, perhaps, unlike that of any other two people in existence. In general, nations not owing a common allegiance are foreign to each other. ... [However, i]n all our intercourse with foreign nations ... [Indians] are considered as within the jurisdictional limits of the United States ... . They occupy a territory to which we assert a title independent of their will." The Cherokee were thus entitled neither to the rights of citizens nor to the privileges due foreign sovereigns.[26]

In adopting this view, the Marshall Court built upon its earlier decision in *Johnson v. M'Intosh* (1823). There, the Court had endorsed the early modern "doctrine of discovery," according to which sovereign territorial rights passed to the European colonial power that had discovered a particular portion of the New World to the exclusion of other European powers. The doctrine of discovery bypassed indigenous populations more or less completely: they were not entitled to the duties one European power owed another. Neither could indigenous populations be incorporated into the new polities created as a result of discovery: their property and territorial rights merited no regard. Under the doctrine of discovery, ruled the Marshall Court, Native Americans had no collective territorial or property rights in land that American courts were compelled to recognize. All they possessed were rights of occupancy, euphemistically called "Indian title," which they held at the pure sufferance of the sovereign.[27] Thus, just as in *Cherokee Nation v. Georgia*, Native Americans were suspended between citizen and alien, undeserving of the respect owed foreign sovereigns and the protections owed citizens.

Even though the Marshall Court attempted to be protective of the rights of Native Americans (at least relative to the eliminationist attitudes of President Andrew Jackson and states like Georgia), tortured decisions such as *Cherokee Nation v. Georgia* and *Johnson v. M'Intosh* were part and parcel of a variegated array of legal and nonlegal responses that effectively rendered Native Americans foreigners in their own lands without benefit of the duties owing to foreigners; stripped them of rights to remain where they were born and had constituted communities for centuries; and ultimately left them vulnerable to removal. The history that followed—the broken treaties, massacres, expulsions, forced relocations—becomes comprehensible in light of such constitutional pronouncements, though it cannot be reduced to them. National territory was cleared for white settlement, *inter alia*, by legally suspending Native Americans between citizenship and alienage.[28]

But the constitutional dilemmas surrounding immigration and citizenship during the antebellum years had directly to do with another—and eventually far more explosive—exclusion: the denial of citizenship and its related rights to African Americans, free and enslaved.

Throughout the antebellum period, both free and slave states adamantly insisted on their ability to exclude alien and native-born free blacks. Even in states that saw themselves as bastions of antislavery sentiment, free blacks remained unwelcome. In 1822, in a report entitled *Free Negroes and Mulattoes*, a Massachusetts legislative committee emphasized "the necessity of checking the increase of a species of population, which threatens to be both injurious and burthensome."[29] States further west sought to oblige blacks seeking residence to provide assurance that they would not become public charges. In other instances, blacks were forbidden to move into the state altogether, sometimes as a result of state constitutional provisions.[30]

The paranoia surrounding the presence of free blacks was, of course, far greater in slave states than in free. In the aftermath of the Haitian Revolution, emancipations in the British empire, and the threat of slave revolts in the South itself, southern states sought to bar free blacks from their territories. In 1822, South Carolina passed an Act for the Better Regulation of Free Negroes and Persons of Color, in which it provided that free blacks on board any vessels entering South Carolina would be "seized and confined in gaol until such vessel shall clear out and depart from this state." The costs of detention were to be paid by ships' captains. The law caused an international incident with Great Britain, which protested the treatment of its subjects of color.[31] As the ideological struggle over slavery intensified, the fears concerning free blacks mounted. Slave-state legislation usually barred the entry of free blacks who were not already state residents; over time, states extended these prohibitions to their own free black residents who sought to return after traveling outside the state either to a disapproved location or in some cases to any destination at all. Slave states also often required that manumitted slaves leave the state forever on pain of reenslavement. Shortly before the Civil War, several slave states considered forcing their free black populations to choose between enslavement and expulsion, legislation that only Arkansas actually passed.[32]

The Court repeatedly acquiesced in free and slave states' attempts to exclude native-born free blacks. According to the Taney Court, state police power authorized setting up internal barriers to the movement of blacks. In *Moore v. Illinois* (1853), Justice Grier reasoned:

> In the exercise of this power, which has been denominated the police power, a State has a right to make it a penal offence to introduce paupers, criminals or fugitive slaves, within their borders ... . Some of the States, coterminous with those who

tolerate slavery, have found it necessary to protect themselves against the influx either of liberated or fugitive slaves, and to repel from their soil a population likely to become burdensome and injurious, either as paupers or criminals.[33]

In acquiescing in states' efforts to exclude native-born free blacks, the Court was also taking a position on native-born free blacks' citizenship and territorial rights. If national citizenship implied a right to travel throughout national territory, as Chief Justice Taney argued in the *Passenger Cases* (1849), then upholding states' right to exclude native-born free blacks from their territories entailed excluding native-born free blacks from national citizenship.[34]

This is precisely the position the Taney Court eventually adopted. The Court's tortured 1857 decision in *Dred Scott v. Sandford* (1857) merely confirmed the awkward suspension of native-born free blacks between the status of citizen and alien. According to Justice Taney's opinion, blacks could not be U.S. citizens by reason of birth on U.S. soil (*jus soli*), birth to a citizen father (*jus sanguinis*), or naturalization.[35] The decision was especially disastrous for those portions of the free black population that had been accorded the status of citizens in certain northern states. In *Dred Scott*, the Court seemed to tell free states that their decision to grant citizenship to their free black populations would have no impact on free blacks' ability to become citizens of the United States.

Given this considerable legal investment in denying black Americans' citizenship and territorial rights, it is not surprising that at least some southern state courts formally assimilated out-of-state free blacks to the status of aliens. This was hardly a common legal position (for the most part, there was satisfaction simply with denying free blacks' citizenship), but it is the ultimate illustration of the internal "foreignness" of native-born free blacks. In the 1859 decision in *Heirn v. Bridault*, the Mississippi Supreme Court ruled that a Louisiana free black woman could not, *as an alien*, inherit the property of a white man with whom she had been cohabiting in Mississippi. It offered the following rationale: "[F]ree negroes [who were in Mississippi in violation of law] are to be regarded as alien enemies or strangers prohibiti, and without the pale of comity, and incapable of acquiring or maintaining property in this State which will be recognized by our courts."[36] In characterizing a native-born black woman as an "alien enemy," incapable of inheriting property, the Mississippi court had done no more than follow through on the implications of *Dred Scott*.

Native-born free blacks' lack of citizenship and territorial rights, and their subjection to internal borders, had a profound impact on the antebellum constitutional jurisprudence of immigration In the 1830s and 1840s, state-level immigration regimes remained oriented as before around the exclusion of the poor (with some additional targeting of immigrants with criminal backgrounds). Although state statutes continued to focus on alien and citizen passengers, mass immigration combined with anti-Catholic sentiment caused the ire of nativists to focus especially on aliens. With the economic panic of the late 1830s, and the consequent problems of immigrant pauperism, the targeting of immigrants ratcheted upwards. States such as Massachusetts and New York eventually started charging per capita fees for passengers landing in their ports, with the collected funds employed to defray the costs of supporting the immigrant poor. The New York statute challenged in the *Passenger Cases* of 1849 set forth a differentiated structure of fees payable to the city's health commissioners, who were directed to use the collected monies to meet the costs of the marine hospital and to turn over all surpluses to the Society for the Reformation of Juvenile Delinquents. According to the fee structure, which reveals how antebellum borders operated against immigrants and natives alike (albeit with heavier burdens placed on immigrants), cabin passengers from foreign ports were taxed at one dollar and fifty cents each; steerage passengers from foreign ports at a dollar each; and passengers on coasting vessels at a rate of twenty-five cents each (with coasting vessels from New Jersey, Connecticut, and Rhode Island required to pay fees no more than once a month). The statute made no mention of citizenship whatsoever, although it was clear that ships from foreign ports were more likely to carry aliens and coasting vessels more likely to carry Americans.

The dispute in the *Passenger Cases* divided the Court sharply. The published arguments and opinions run almost 300 pages in the *United States Reports* and consist of seven lengthy opinions (including three rambling dissents). The formal constitutional question was couched in terms of whether Congress possessed the power to exclude and remove noncitizens from national territory pursuant to Article 1, Section 8, of the Constitution, which gave it the authority "to regulate Commerce with foreign Nations, and among the several States," or whether the states possessed a corresponding power as part of their regular and residual police power to promote the health, safety, and welfare of their populations.

In *Mayor of the City of New York v. Miln* (1837), its only previous examination of the constitutionality of state immigration statutes, the Court had upheld a New York law requiring shipmasters to report passenger information and post bonds for passengers who might become chargeable as paupers to New York City; the statute had not, however, required fees.[37] The Court had grounded its decision on a rather simple territorial logic. New York was not interfering with the transportation of passengers, which was subject to Congress' foreign commerce power, but only mitigating fiscal problems associated with passengers who had landed in New York, which fell within the purview of New York's police power. Distinguishing this case from two of the Marshall Court's great Commerce Clause cases, *Gibbons v. Ogden* (1824) and *Brown v. Maryland* (1827), Justice Thompson endorsed the New York law as a legitimate exercise of the state's police power and as no interference with Congress' Commerce Clause powers:

> For although commerce, within the sense of the constitution may mean intercourse, and the power to regulate it be co-extensive with the subject on which it acts ... it cannot be claimed, that the master [of the ship], or the passengers, are exempted from the duty imposed by the laws of a state, after their arrival within its jurisdiction; or have a right to wander, uncontrolled, after they become mixed with the general population of the state; or that any greater rights or privileges attach to them, because they come in through the medium of navigation, than if they come by land from an adjoining state ... .

A little later in his opinion, Justice Thompson asked rhetorically: "Can anything fall more directly within the police power and internal regulation of a state, than that which concerns the care and management of paupers or convicts ... ?"[38]

When the *Passenger Cases* came up for decision a mere twelve years later, a majority of the members of the Court was deeply troubled by New York's and Massachusetts' taxes on incoming passengers. Although they had acquiesced in New York's requirement of bonds in *Miln*, the taxes in these later immigration statutes seemed to go much further, representing a clear interference with Congress' foreign and interstate commerce powers (although only the former was at issue in the cases). New York and Massachusetts appeared to be taxing navigation. But the justices were also acutely aware of how any Supreme Court decision scaling back states' rights to control access to their territories would be read by an ever-vigilant and increasingly paranoid South. Justice Wayne sought to assure the South explicitly that the Court's decision striking down the New York and Massachusetts laws should not be a cause for concern:

> The fear expressed, that if the States have not the discretion to determine who may come and live in them, the United States may introduce into the Southern States emancipated negroes from the West Indies and elsewhere, has no foundation. ...
>
> [S]hould this matter of introducing free negroes into the Southern States ever become the subject of judicial inquiry, ... they have a guard against it in the Constitution, making it altogether unnecessary for them to result to the *casus gentis extraordinarius*,

the *casus extremae necessitatis* of nations, for their protection and preservation. They may rely upon the Constitution, and the correct interpretation of it, without seeking to be relieved from any of their obligations under it, or having recourse to the *jus necessitatis* for self-preservation.[39]

Highly solicitous of states' rights views (and particularly of their pro-slavery iterations), the justices took care to signal that in striking down the alien passenger taxes, they were *not* interfering with state police powers to regulate access to their territories: states could continue to demand securities to indemnify the public from costs associated with immigrant pauperism, as they had in *Miln*. State police power encompassed the right to control pauperism *and* the presence of blacks. State immigration regimes, founded on state police powers, would thus continue unchecked. Justice Wayne put it thus:

> But I have said the States have the right to turn off paupers, vagabonds, and fugitives from justice, and the States where slaves are have a constitutional right to exclude all such as are, from a common ancestry and country, of the same class of men. And when Congress shall legislate ... to make paupers, vagabonds, suspected persons, and fugitives from justice subjects of admission into the United States, I do not doubt it will be found and declared ... that such persons are not within the regulating power which the United States have over commerce.[40]

It should come as no surprise, then, that the *Passenger Cases* were dead on arrival. Even as the Court sought to follow the logic of the Commerce Clause, and limit the regulatory authority of the states over immigration, it felt simultaneously compelled to insist upon the sacrosanct status of state police powers to regulate the presence of outsiders in their own territories. This insistence on state power (a great deal of which had do with pressure from the slave states) meant that northern immigrant-receiving states continued to have the right to request bonds from incoming passengers, even if they could not impose taxes or fees. New York and Massachusetts circumvented the Court's ruling instantly, demanding bonds of all passengers, but offering shipmasters the option to commute those bonds by paying a fee instead. The fee levels remained at exactly the same level as that of the taxes struck down in the *Passenger Cases*. New York, Massachusetts, and other states thus went on regulating immigration and collecting funds, just as the slave states continued to regulate black Americans' access to their territories.

The antebellum world of variegated and plural legalities and memberships was a world in which immigrants were thus not the only individuals visited with the disabilities associated with a lack of citizenship. Furthermore, the fractured legal landscape gave immigrants room to maneuver: if Massachusetts' bonding requirements were too stringent, for instance, immigrants could simply land in New York and travel overland, thereby escaping Massachusetts' port authorities. But for all its plurality and fracture, we should be wary of assuming that this was a better world for immigrants. In the hands of the states, there was a small amount of transatlantic deportation traffic. Massachusetts figures for the mid-1850s were as follows: 1,537 removals in 1855 (286 to Liverpool); 1,358 removals in 1856 (193 to Liverpool); 3,267 removals in 1858 (342 to Liverpool).[41] These numbers, though small, are troubling because there appears to have been a certain disregard of procedural protections owing to the immigrants removed under the aegis of Massachusetts' police power. 1n 1855, Peleg Chandler, one of Massachusetts' newly created Alien Commissioners, complained about the practice of deporting lunatic immigrant paupers and questioned state officials' accounts that they had undertaken the removals at the request of the immigrants themselves. Chandler complained:

> Since the commencement of the present year, paupers have been taken from one of the lunatic hospitals and sent over the sea to their alleged homes, and this at the expense of the State, but without any complaint to a justice of the peace ... . It is said that these people *consented* to go. *The consent of lunatics!* When it is one of the wisest and most humane maxims of the law that a lunatic can give no consent to anything.

A legislative committee of the Massachusetts' General Court, then under the control of the nativist Know-Nothing Party, found Chandler's charges groundless. The committee observed: "Sympathy appears to be wasted altogether upon the matter ... . It may be said that the whole life and being of the confirmed pauper is almost purely animal, and often of a degraded character even in that classification. ... [T]here is nothing in this course that approaches to persecution or injustice."[42]

The Era of Racial Restriction:
Immigration, Citizenship, and the Constitution from the Civil War to the Mid-Twentieth Century

The Civil War resolved the most egregious instance of the antebellum era's uneven distribution of citizenship among the native-born population. In 1868, expressly with a view to overruling the *Dred Scott* decision, Congress wrote the principle of *jus soli* or birthright citizenship into the Fourteenth Amendment to the Constitution: "All persons born or naturalized in the United States, and subject to the jurisdiction thereof, are citizens of the United States and of the state wherein they reside."[43] From this point on, U.S. citizenship was defined as a matter of the birth or naturalization of a "person" in the United States. A feudal principle with its origins in the allegiance owing from vassal to lord became a pillar in the enfranchisement of freedmen.

The consequences were profound. Native-born blacks would never again be denied citizenship, suspended between the legal status of citizen and alien or, worse yet, formally assimilated to the status of aliens as they had in some slave states just prior to the outbreak of the war. Neither could states withhold state citizenship from them. The Fourteenth Amendment reversed the valences of state and national citizenship definitively. Henceforth, national citizenship would be primary, with state citizenship following as a mere function of where a national citizen resided. These developments, combined with the end of slavery, expanded the community of United States citizens overnight by millions.[44]

Exceptions marred the clarity of the new birthright citizenship principle. As interpreted by the Court in *Elk v. Wilkins* (1884), the Fourteenth Amendment did not extend birthright citizenship to Native Americans. The words "subject to the jurisdiction thereof," the Court held, "mean not merely in some respect or degree to the jurisdiction of the United States, but completely subject to their political jurisdiction, and owing them direct and immediate allegiance." Most Native Americans failed this test: "Indians born within the territorial limits of the United States, members of, and owing immediate allegiance to, one of the Indian tribes, (an alien though dependent power,) although in a geographic sense born in the United States, are no more 'born in the United States and subject to the jurisdiction thereof,' ... than the children of subjects of any foreign government born within the domain of that government."[45] In other words, Native Americans born within U.S. territory as members of tribes were, according to the Court's reading of the Fourteenth Amendment's birthright citizenship clause, like Frenchmen born in France. Congress would need to pass legislation to overcome this holding.[46]

Populations of territories acquired by the United States after the Spanish-American War of 1898 constituted another exception to the Fourteenth Amendment's birthright citizenship clause. In the early twentieth century, in a series of decisions known as the *Insular Cases*, the Court struggled with questions of what constitutional protections and personal status accrued to residents of the newly acquired territories, finally deciding on a somewhat reduced level of constitutional protection in those territories because they were not incorporated into the United States and simultaneously concluding that their inhabitants were not citizens. of the United States but merely "nationals."[47] Eventually, Congress either granted full citizenship to the local population, as in the case of Puerto Rico, or passed legislation granting the territory independence, as was the case for the Philippines.[48]

These exceptions apart, as U.S. citizenship was placed above state citizenship and formally extended to the entire native-born population, it began to make sense to conceive of national territory as a space of and for a coherent and inclusive community of U.S. citizens in a way that had simply not been possible in the antebellum period. Internal borders set up to control the movement of black Americans prior to the Civil War fell away. There were gestures towards constitutionalizing the right to travel throughout U.S. territory as an incident of U.S. citizenship. In *Crandall v. Nevada* (1867), the Court struck down a Nevada tax on persons leaving the state by means of public transportation on the ground that national citizenship encompassed the right to travel from state to state. Although this decision did not attempt to bring state legal restrictions on the territorial mobility of the native-born poor to an end, it became the first significant constitutional pronouncement that set the stage for their long decline.[49]

Together, these developments enabled the emergence of a national immigration regime that could turn its gaze exclusively outwards upon noncitizen immigrants. The postwar United States was no longer a society peopled by citizens and classes of native-born permanent noncitizens who could be kept from entering and residing in certain parts of national territory. The international border was no longer chopped up among a host of sovereigns jealously guarding access to their territories. It made sense, then, to shift immigration restriction to the national level, for borders to move outwards until they became coterminous with the nation's international borders. It was no accident that the state-level immigration regimes that had survived constitutional scrutiny in the *Passenger Cases* (1849) were declared unconstitutional relatively soon after slavery's demise.[50] In the last third of the nineteenth century, a federal immigration order emerged.

The organizing principle of the constitutional architecture of this new federal immigration order was plenary power, and it developed in the course of the federal government's dealings with Chinese immigrants. Men and women from China had been immigrating to the United States since the late 1840s. Initially, a current of pro-Chinese sentiment coalesced around appreciation for Chinese labor, on the one hand, and the desire to increase commercial contact with China, on the other. In 1868, the United States and China signed the Burlingame Treaty, which recognized reciprocal rights of travel "for purposes of curiosity, of trade, or as permanent residents."[51] But anti-Chinese sentiment grew in California and began to seep into national attitudes. In 1875, as the very first piece of federal immigration legislation, Congress passed the Page Law, aimed at excluding "coolie labor" and Chinese prostitutes.[52]

As the move to restrict the entry of Chinese immigrants became a key issue in the national election of 1880, the United States renegotiated the Burlingame Treaty to give itself the right to "regulate, limit or suspend" the immigration of Chinese laborers whenever their entry or residence in the United States "affects or threatens to affect the interests of that country, or to endanger the good order of [the United States] or of any locality within the territory thereof."[53] Shortly thereafter, in 1882, Congress enacted the first of a series of Chinese exclusion laws suspending the immigration of Chinese laborers.[54] For the first time in its history, as a matter of formal law, the United States denied individuals the right to enter the country on the ground of race or nationality.

When these laws were challenged in the *Chinese Exclusion Case*, the Court began to articulate what would become known in immigration law as the plenary power doctrine. Although it acknowledged that the 1888 law under challenge was in fact in conflict with the treaty with China, the Court decided that it had no authority to curb Congress' power to exclude aliens, regardless of the injustices inflicted upon them. It expressed itself as follows: "The power of exclusion of foreigners being an incident of sovereignty belonging to the government of the United States, as part of the sovereign powers delegated by the Constitution, the right to its exercise at any time when, in the judgment of the government, the interests of the country require it, cannot be granted away or restrained on behalf of any one."[55] The assertion that the exclusion of foreigners was a sovereign right was not new. As we have seen, it was part of international law theory, going back to the eighteenth century. What was new was that this was now asserted as a right belonging to the federal government as an incident of sovereignty, and *not* as part of its Commerce power. Grounded in sovereignty rather than in one of Congress' enumerated powers, the power was rendered immune from substantive judicial review.

From its decision to immunize from substantive judicial review the federal government's power to exclude entering immigrants, the Court moved to immunize the federal power to deport resident immigrants. The 1892 Geary Act provided for the deportation of resident aliens. All Chinese laborers living in the United States were required to obtain a "certificate of residence" from the Collector of Internal Revenue within one year of the act's passage. Under regulations promulgated pursuant to the 1892 Act, the government would issue a certificate only on the "affidavit of at least one credible [white] witness." Any Chinese alien who failed to obtain the certificate could be "arrested ... and taken before a United States judge, whose duty it [was] to order that he be deported from the United States."[56]

The Geary Act sparked a campaign for noncompliance led by the Chinese Six Companies, the leading Chinese immigrant organization of the day, who set up a test case. It reached the Court, and met with defeat. In *Fong Yue Ting v. United States* (1893), the Court declared that "[t]he right of a nation to expel or deport foreigners, who have not been naturalized or taken any steps towards becoming citizens of the country, rests upon the same grounds, and is as absolute and unqualified as the right to prohibit and prevent their entrance into the country." Even worse, the Court ruled that deportation "is not a punishment for a crime," but only "a method of enforcing the return to his own country of an alien." Interpreting deportation as a civil, rather than a criminal, sanction denied the deported alien the constitutional protections available to criminal defendants.[57] Deportation was thus also made immune from substantive judicial review.

The final area to which the plenary power doctrine applied was naturalization law. If Chinese immigrants were to be physically excluded and removed from national territory, they were also to be denied access to the polity. In the aftermath of the Civil War, Congress had moved to amend the naturalization statute restricting naturalization to "free white persons" in order to make naturalization available to individuals of African descent. In 1870, Senator Charles Sumner of Massachusetts had proposed that Congress simply delete references to "white" in the naturalization law, thereby opening up the possibility of citizenship to all immigrants regardless of race, but congressmen from the western states had defeated his proposal on the ground that it would permit Chinese immigrants to become citizens. Accordingly, in keeping with the anti-slavery sentiments of the Reconstruction Congress, naturalization was extended only to "aliens of African nativity and to persons of African descent."[58] Attorneys petitioning for naturalization on behalf of Chinese immigrants subsequently argued that the term "white" in the 1870 naturalization law was poorly defined, and should be interpreted to include people of Chinese descent. The federal courts disagreed, however, on the grounds that white people were part of Caucasian race and that Chinese were of the "Mongolian race."[59] Congress then explicitly excluded Chinese immigrants from naturalization through the Chinese exclusion laws. This would be an authoritative legal position until the mid-twentieth century.

By 1900, not only had the federal government assumed control over the regulation and administration of immigration and dislodged the states, it had been assured by the Court that under the plenary power doctrine the Constitution would not be interpreted as a substantive barrier to exclusion, deportation, and naturalization laws. If legal scholars are wont to think of the years around 1900 as the high noon of substantive due process, when the police powers of government were fettered by the constitutionalization of rights to property and contract in cases such as *Lochner v. New York* (1905), this was also an era in which unfettered governmental power achieved great license, freed by the Court to create strong distinctions between citizens and aliens, insiders and outsiders.[60]

Yet the very harshness of the plenary power doctrine led to the invigoration of different sets of legal distinctions—the territorial inside/outside distinction and the procedure/substance distinction—that had the effect of softening that harshness. Even as the Court authorized the drawing of strong distinctions between citizens and aliens by immunizing the immigration and naturalization power from substantive constitutional review, it undermined those distinctions in diverse ways, thereby restoring a modicum of parity between citizens and aliens.

First, with respect to the territorial inside/outside distinction, the Court made clear that various provisions of the Constitution protected all "persons"— in other words, citizens *and* noncitizens—who happened to be on the territorial inside. In 1898, despite arguments from the government to the contrary, the Court held that the Fourteenth Amendment's embrace of "persons" in its birthright citizenship clause ensured that all native-born Chinese would be U.S. citizens.[61] If Congress could keep Chinese immigrants out of the polity through its plenary power over naturalization laws, it would not be able to withhold citizenship from individuals of Chinese descent born within U.S. territory.

Those physically present within the territory of the United States were also able to protest discriminatory treatment by the states under the Equal Protection Clause of the Fourteenth Amendment and to demand the protections afforded by the Due Process Clause of the Fifth Amendment when the federal government sought to punish them for violating immigration laws.[62] The constitutional commitment to protecting all "persons" who happened to be inside U.S. territory never interfered with the federal government's basic power to exclude and deport, which continued to be treated under the plenary power doctrine. Thus, detention incident to deportation was covered by the plenary power doctrine, while detention visited as a punishment upon territorially present immigrants had to be accompanied by constitutionally required procedural protections.

Second, the procedure/substance distinction came to afford immigrants a measure of protection, especially when it linked to the immigrant's stake in American society. As the federal government's substantive power to exclude and deport aliens was progressively immunized from judicial review under the plenary power doctrine, immigrants' strategies focused increasingly on procedural issues. From its inception, the Chinese community in San Francisco proved adept at seeking out judicial assistance in curbing the excesses of overzealous immigration officials. Despite federal judges' opposition to Chinese immigration generally, they often used their *habeas corpus* jurisdiction to overturn immigration officials' decisions to exclude Chinese immigrants, thereby leading to considerable tension between courts and bureaucrats, with the latter accusing the former of subverting the administration of the Chinese exclusion laws. In 1891, Congress created a federal superintendent of immigration, whose decisions would be subject to review by the secretary of the treasury.[63] In response to the complaints of immigration officials, the 1891 act also made decisions of immigration inspection officers final. Appeals could be taken to the superintendent of immigration and then to the secretary of the treasury, with judicial review of administrative decisions eliminated for entering immigrants. In 1891, a Japanese immigrant denied admission on the ground that she would become a public charge challenged the procedural arrangements of the 1891 act as a denial of due process. The Court dismissed her claims.[64]

Nevertheless, in the context of an alien threatened with deportation, the Court gestured towards a constitutional requirement of due process. *The Japanese Immigrant Case (Yamataya v. Fisher)* (1903) involved the deportation, rather than the exclusion, of an alien. The alien in question was deportable on the ground that she had been excludable at the time of entry as likely to become a public charge, but had nevertheless been allowed to enter. She alleged various procedural defects: the investigation had been conducted in English (which she did not understand); she had not realized that the investigation involved deportability; she had not been assisted by counsel; and she had never been given the opportunity to demonstrate that she was not deportable. Astonishingly, the Court found none of these specific procedural defects to be constitutionally fatal, and she lost. Nevertheless, it found that due process was required in the context of deportation:

[I]t is not competent for the Secretary of the Treasury or any executive officer ... arbitrarily to cause an alien, who has entered the country, and has become subject in all respects to its jurisdiction, and a part of its population, although alleged to be illegally here, to be taken into custody and deported without giving him all opportunity to be heard upon the questions involving his right to be and remain in the United States. No such arbitrary power can exist where the principles involved in due process of law are recognized.[65]

Thus, the immigrant's presence within territory, and her increased ties with American society, triggered additional procedural protections when the government sought to deport her. The Court recognized that over time, territorially present immigrants might acquire a stake in American society and slowly become insiders themselves.

By 1900, the restrictionist focus had shifted far beyond the Chinese. The United States was in the grip of a mass immigration that dwarfed all previous immigration streams. Half of all those who arrived between the War of 1812 and the Great Depression did so during the years from between 1900 and 1925. They came increasingly from southern and eastern Europe, rather than from northern and western Europe as had been the case for much of the nineteenth century. Nevertheless, it was the legal struggles of Chinese immigrants that brought about an articulation of the major principles of the federal immigration order, These include racialized citizenship; plenary congressional power over the exclusion, deportation, and naturalization of immigrants; broad judicial deference to administrative decisions; and a judicial effort to undermine the harshness of plenary power through the invocation of the territorial inside/outside distinction and the procedure/substance distinction.

As the federal immigration regime consolidated itself, the grounds for exclusion multiplied. The anxieties expressed by the state in its exclusion laws typified the punitive, moralizing, reformist, and eugenicist mood of the late nineteenth and early twentieth centuries. Where constitutional strictures might occasionally have restrained government in the context of domestic law, Congress could be confident that, under the aegis of the plenary power doctrine, it could proceed relatively unfettered when it came to immigrants. The exclusion of those "likely to become a public charge," a provision enacted in 1882 and based on antebellum state statutes drawing upon the poor laws, became the most important ground for barring entry into the United States.[66] As historian Margot Canaday has shown, the public charge provision could be invoked for a range of purposes, including the exclusion of those whose identities fell outside heteronormative standards.[67] Closely related were laws restricting the admission of aliens with physical and mental defects, including epileptics and alcoholics, which drove prospective entrants to conceal limps and coughs.[68] Laws targeted individuals with criminal backgrounds (including those convicted of crimes involving "moral turpitude"), polygamists, and women coming to the United States for "immoral purposes."[69] Finally, following the assassination of President McKinley in 1901, immigration laws began actively to penalize aliens for their political beliefs.[70]

The heart of the debate over immigration restriction in the early twentieth century, however, lay elsewhere—not in the protection of the labor market, public finances, public morals, or the polity itself, but in something that stood in the popular mind for all of these together—protection of the country's ethnic/racial stock. Increasingly, the race of immigrants did the work of "explaining" the class tensions, labor unrest, and urban violence afflicting late nineteenth- and early twentieth-century America. The fear of "race suicide"—allegedly committed by those of "Nordic" descent but hastened by admission of more prolific "inferior races"—acquired considerable currency after 1900, propagated energetically by the eastern elite-dominated Immigration Restriction League. The massive report on immigration submitted to Congress by the Dillingham Commission shared this general sensibility and considerately included a *Dictionary of Races or Peoples*. The *Dictionary* exemplified the new "scientific" understanding of race. Classifying immigrants "according to their languages, their physical characteristics, and such marks as would show their relationship to one another, and in determining their geographical habitats," the commission identified dozens of carefully hierarchized "races."[71] But significant restrictions on immigration awaited the xenophobic frenzy whipped up during the First World War.

The suspicion fostered by the war enabled nativists to obtain, in the Immigration Act of 1917, some of the restrictionist policies they had long advocated. The 1917 law yielded to the West Coast's demands for the exclusion of Indian immigrants. Hesitant to single Indians out for exclusion on the grounds of race, Congress created an "Asiatic Barred Zone" that included India, Burma, Siam, the Malay States, Arabia, Afghanistan, parts of Russia, and most of the Polynesian Islands.[72] In addition, a literacy test for adult immigrants was one of the nativists' most important victories. In the end, it is unclear how much the literacy test affected immigration from Europe, in part because of the spread of literacy in Europe during the same years.

By 1920, the war-boom economy had begun to collapse and immigration from Europe had revived, creating a propitious environment for greater restriction. Accordingly, in 1921, the logic of immigration restriction applicable to almost all Asian immigrants since 1917—namely, exclusion—was extended to European immigrants, albeit in the form of quotas rather than complete exclusion. The Quota Act of 1921 limited European immigration to 3 percent of all foreign-born people of each nationality residing in the United States in

1910.[73] The aim was to give larger quotas to immigrants from northern and western Europe, and to reduce the influx of southern and eastern Europeans. This change failed to satisfy nativists. The Immigration Act of 1924 represented a compromise. The act reduced the percentage admitted from 3 to 2, making the base population the number of each foreign-born nationality present in the United States in 1890 instead of 1910, which would reduce the southern and eastern European quotas even further. Balking at such arrant discrimination, the Senate allowed the new quota provided that a new "national origins" test be used beginning in 1927. The new test was only superficially fairer. It placed a cap on the total number of immigrants, limiting admissions to 150,000 each year and using the 1920 census as the base. However, instead of using the number of foreign-born as its measure, in the manner of earlier quotas, quotas were now set according to the proportion of each "national stock," including both native and foreign-born people. This once again favored "old stock" Americans over the new immigrant population—leaving to immigration officials the nightmare of calculating "national stocks." The 1924 act also furthered the exclusion of Asians. Though the law barred from entry all aliens "ineligible for citizenship," Japanese immigrants were the real targets of the act because Chinese, Indian, and other Asian immigrants had already been excluded.[74]

Immigration from the Western Hemisphere remained the major exception to restriction in this period. Of the three principal sources of Western Hemisphere immigration (Canada, Mexico, and Puerto Rico), Mexico was by far the most significant. Principally because of the particular history of the way in which Mexican territory had been incorporated into the United States, Mexican immigrants were not barred from naturalizing. In 1897, a federal district court considering the question of Mexicans' eligibility for citizenship declared that "if the strict scientific classification of the anthropologist should be adopted, [the petitioner] would probably not be classed as white." However, the constitution of the Texas Republic, the Treaty of Guadalupe Hidalgo, and other agreements between the United States and Mexico either "affirmatively confer[red] the rights of citizenship upon Mexicans, or tacitly recognize[d] in them the right of individual naturalization."[75] Pressure from agricultural lobbies in western states also kept Western Hemisphere immigration free from categorical bans and quotas, a phenomenon the political scientist Aristide Zolberg has referred to as the "back door" of the American immigration system.[76]

Aside from this "back door," the basic theory of exclusion shifted in the 1920s from considering the shortcomings of the individual immigrant (poverty, criminal background, health, etc.) to a matter of numerical restriction. Of course, the grounds of exclusion for poverty, disability, criminal background, political opinion, and the like would continue in force, but these would henceforth serve to weed out individuals who had first to demonstrate that they fit within a national origins quota. The presumption that one could immigrate to the United States had shifted to a presumption that one could not. With this shift came the figure of the "illegal alien" and a vast surge of border control and deportation activity. In 1925, for the first time, Congress legislated a serious enforcement mechanism against unlawful entry by creating a land Border Patrol.[77]

As the composition of the immigrant population changed, courts were compelled to confront once again the question of racial ineligibility to U.S. citizenship. Although Chinese immigrants had been declared ineligible for citizenship since the 1870s, considerable ambiguity remained as to whether Japanese, Indian, and other immigrants who entered the United States in the late nineteenth and early twentieth centuries fit within the black-white binary of naturalization law. Between 1887 and 1923, the federal courts heard twenty-five cases challenging racial prerequisites to citizenship, culminating in two rulings by the Court, *Ozawa v. United States* (1922) and *Thind v. United States* (1923).[78] In each case, the Court's decision turned on whether the petitioner could be considered a "white person" within the meaning of the statute.

Taken together, these decisions reveal the shortcomings of racial "science." In earlier years, federal courts had relied on racial "science," rather than upon color, and had admitted Syrians, Armenians, and Indians to citizenship as "white persons." In *Ozawa*, the U.S. Supreme Court admitted that color as an indicator of race was insufficient, but resisted the conclusion that no scientific grounds for race existed. It elided the problem of classification by asserting that "white" and Caucasian were the same, and that the Japanese were not Caucasian and hence not "white."[79] The Court was then confronted, in *Thind*, with an Indian immigrant who staked his claim to citizenship on the basis of his Aryan and Caucasian roots. Now the Court found "Caucasian" to be considerably broader in scientific discourses than it was in nonscientific discourses. Rejecting the petitioner's claim to citizenship, it held that the words "white person" in the naturalization law were words of "common speech, to be interpreted with the understanding of the common man."[80] Racial "science" was summarily abandoned in favor of popular prejudice.

If U.S. citizenship was racialized during this period, it was also deeply gendered. Since the middle of the nineteenth century, male U.S. citizens had been able to confer citizenship upon their wives. However, the law with respect to female U.S. citizens who married noncitizens had been unclear. In 1907, Congress decided to remove all ambiguities by legislating "that any American woman who marries a foreigner shall take the nationality of her husband."[81] In other words, female U.S. citizens who married noncitizens were not only unable to confer citizenship upon their husbands, but lost their own U.S. citizenship. In 1915, the Court upheld a challenge to this provision on the basis of the "ancient principle" of "the identity of husband and wife."[82] The law rendered native-born Asian American female citizens who married aliens permanently unable to reenter the community of citizens: having lost their citizenship by marrying an alien, they became aliens racially ineligible for citizenship. Penalizing marriages between male aliens and female citizens through denaturalization of female spouses was abolished in 1922 by the Cable Act, which granted "independent citizenship for married women." Henceforth, no female citizen could lose her citizenship by marriage to an alien. But explicit gender discrimination persisted when it came to citizenship *jure sanguinis*, or citizenship transmitted through blood. Until 1934, statutory law allowed the transmission of U.S. citizenship by American fathers, but not American mothers.

In the early twentieth century, quite in addition to being racialized and gendered, U.S. citizenship became potent weapon of discrimination in the hands of state legislatures. As anti-immigrant sentiment mounted, U.S. citizenship was made a prerequisite to an increasing number of jobs, types of recreation, and access to natural resources, thereby causing the meanings of citizenship to proliferate well beyond the formal political sphere. Driven by the politics of race and labor, citizenship spilled into the social experiences of work and leisure in the lived community. The Court typically dealt with state attempts to discriminate on the basis of citizenship as problems of "alienage law." In *Barbier v. Connolly* (1885), the Court held that a state could enact laws discriminating between citizens and aliens as a matter of state police power, as long as it did not interfere with Congress' now exclusive power over immigration.[83] As its alienage jurisprudence developed, the Court held that a state could discriminate among citizens and aliens if the state was protecting a "special public interest" in its common property or resources, a category that was interpreted over the years to include employment on public works projects, hunting wild game, and operating pool halls. Almost all states barred aliens from practicing law, and many excluded aliens from architecture, engineering, surveying, medicine, dentistry, optometry, and other health professions.[84]

The Court also upheld alienage distinctions that were very clearly directly targeted at specific, racialized immigrant groups. In the early twentieth century, resentment of Japanese immigrants on the West Coast increasingly centered on their success in agriculture. In response, Arizona, California, Idaho, Kansas, Louisiana, Montana, New Mexico, and Oregon attempted to restrict land ownership by aliens "ineligible to citizenship," a category carefully crafted to apply to Asian immigrants, the only ones legally incapable of naturalizing. When challenged, the Court upheld alien land laws.[85] The fact that such laws only affected some racialized groups was not found to be a problem under the Equal Protection Clause of the Fourteenth Amendment because the laws was framed in neutral terms.

The harshness of the federal immigration and citizenship laws, together with state discriminatory laws, had the effect of making Asian Americans internal foreigners in early twentieth-century America. Here is one concrete instance in which the denial of citizenship (in the sense of the distinction between citizen and alien) blended into the denial of citizenship (in the sense of internal membership in the polity) and vice versa. Starting in 1909, all persons of Chinese descent—including U.S. citizens of Chinese background—were required to carry certificates identifying them as legally present in the country.[86] As deportation became a common tool of regulation, Chinese communities across the U.S. repeatedly found themselves subjected to what has since become an established method of ferreting out "illegal aliens" and of impressing upon certain kinds of citizens their lack of belonging, namely the immigration raid, with all the possibilities of intimidation and corruption that it carried. The history of Japanese immigrants reveals similar patterns. Prevented from naturalizing, the Issei—the foreign-born first generation of Japanese Americans—were simply unable to remove formal ties of loyalty to and association with Japan. Being barred from a range of professions exacerbated their inability to assimilate. When World War II came, the alienage of Japanese immigrants deepened xenophobic reactions to them. Along with their children, the Nisei (who, albeit citizens, were regarded as children of an enemy race), the Issei were evicted without due process from their homes on the West Coast and interned in relocation camps.[87]

By the mid-twentieth century, the fabled Golden Door welcoming immigrants to the U.S. had effectively closed. The "world-wide welcome" that Emma Lazarus had written about with so much flourish had been largely withdrawn and was paid little heed in the midst of global turmoil. From 1930 until the end of World War II, a combination of factors—the institution of national origins quotas, the worldwide depression, and then the war—caused the number of immigrants to the United States to drop considerably. Indeed, because of the Great Depression and the war, large portions of annual quotas for immigrants went unfilled. From 1930 to the end of World War II, fewer than 700,000 immigrants entered the country, as compared with 5.4 million in the decade and a half before 1930. Only a quarter of all immigrant quotas were actually used. Indeed, during the 1930s, more people left than entered the United States.

A Rights Revolution?
Immigration and Citizenship Law in the Post-World War II Period

The postwar jurisprudence of the Court has traditionally been interpreted in terms of the Court's shift from the substantive due process of the early twentieth century—exemplified by the case of *Lochner v. New York* (1905)—to the protection of rights listed in the Bill of Rights and the rights of "discrete and insular minorities" excluded from the political process, an idea first expressed in *United States v. Carolene Products* (1938).[88] This shift revolutionized citizenship understood as internal membership in diverse contexts including civil, voting, privacy, criminal, and welfare rights. The right to travel throughout national territory, of special interest here, was strongly reaffirmed. The forms of eighteenth- and nineteenth-century spatial restrictions imposed on the domestic poor disappeared. In *Edwards v. California* (1941), the Court struck down a California statute making it a crime to bring an indigent person into the state as an unconstitutional interference with Congress' power to regulate interstate commerce.[89] In *Shapiro v. Thompson* (1969), the Court struck down a Connecticut statute that imposed a one-year waiting period before residents from other states could collect state welfare benefits; the statute was found to interfere with the right to travel, and fell afoul of the Equal Protection Clause of the Fourteenth Amendment.[90]

When it came to federal authority over immigration and naturalization, however, the postwar Court continued to cleave to the late nineteenth-century plenary power doctrine. Immigration and naturalization thus remained outliers relative to post-World War II constitutional jurisprudence more generally. As in the early twentieth century, but more pointedly, the Court undermined plenary power through the invocation of a variety of legal distinctions (substance versus procedure, presence or absence from territory, degree of connection to the United States). In more recent years, the Court has gone a bit further, hinting obliquely that substantive provisions of the Constitution might apply to the federal immigration and naturalization power. The most significant change at the constitutional level has been the Court's willingness to use a combination of preemption and Equal Protection notions to invalidate state laws discriminating between citizens and aliens. In striking down state laws, the Court has accomplished a further federalization of immigration while simultaneously mandating a measure of parity between citizens and aliens.

Despite the relative passivity of the Court vis-à-vis federal immigration and naturalization laws after the Second World War, both changed dramatically in the postwar period. From the horrors provoked by Nazi and Japanese wartime activities to the seemingly unstoppable anti-colonial and anti-racist struggles at home and abroad to initial alliance and then competition with the Soviet Union, it was hard for postwar Americans not to see that the essential order of things was changing. During the war itself, as the United States prepared to assume a new international role, American lawmakers began to think of immigration and naturalization policy as a tool to further American self-interest and reflect changing conceptions of America's relationship with other nations. In 1943, as part of its wartime alliance with China, Congress repealed the Chinese Exclusion Act of 1882. In 1946, it established naturalization rights for Filipinos and admitted aliens from India; racial bars to naturalization were lifted in these acts.[91]

Immigration flows created by the war also placed considerable pressure on the 1920s quota system, resulting in its being abandoned bit by bit. Between 1938 and 1941, the federal government had generally turned its back on war refugees. In 1945, for the first time, President Truman issued an executive order admitting 40,000 refugees and displaced persons. However, when Congress passed legislation to deal with refugees—the Displaced Persons Act of 1948—it required "quota mortgaging," such that refugee admissions were used to fill established country quotas. This policy came under swift and heavy criticism. In response, in 1953, Congress passed the Refugee Relief Act, which provided for 205,000 nonquota refugee visas. The quota system was also abandoned when it came to preserving the families of military personnel who had married overseas. In 1945, Congress passed the War Brides Act, enabling alien wives, husbands, and children of armed services members to enter the United States irrespective of quotas.[92]

But the first major piece of postwar immigration legislation preserved the 1920s quota system. In 1952, over President Truman's veto, Congress passed the voluminous McCarran-Walter Act, which retained the quota structure of the 1920s and awarded northern and western European nations 85 percent of annual admissions while capping slots for the Eastern Hemisphere at 150,000. Immigration from the Western Hemisphere remained free from numerical limits, albeit governed by regimes such as the wartime *bracero* program. In one important respect, however, the McCarran-Walter Act broke from the older model of race as a bar to admission. Culminating the trend begun by the wartime acts ending Chinese and Indian exclusion, the act abolished the closed-door principle when it came to immigrants from Asian countries. Racial bars to naturalization were also lifted: the category of "aliens ineligible for citizenship" was removed from the statute books.

At the same time, the act placed increasing pressure on those suspected of Communist affiliation, prohibiting the naturalization of members of various subversive groups. It also and for the first time introduced a special ground of exclusion and deportation for aliens afflicted with a psychopathic personality, an imprecise way of keeping out homosexuals.[93] The McCarran-Walter Act was a product of the early phase of the Cold War: the United States lifted racial bars to immigration and naturalization to forge alliances worldwide and to defend itself from charges of hypocrisy leveled by the Soviet bloc, even as it sought to purge itself of Communists.[94]

According to the logic of plenary power, the substantive grounds of exclusion and deportation in the McCarran-Walter Act remained immune from constitutional attack. But by mid-century, the Court began explicitly to recognize that outsiders slowly became insiders and that, accordingly, the levels of substantive and procedural protection owing to them increased. This was potentially a way of mitigating the harshness of plenary power. In *Johnson v. Eisentrager* (1950), the Court observed that an alien "is accorded a generous and ascending scale of rights as he increases his identity with our society."[95] Following this logic, an alien's stake in society presumably increased as he or she moved from the context of exclusion (where the alien might be seeking entry or rights to permanent residence within territory) to that of deportation (where the alien might be a legal permanent resident with many years of residence) to that of naturalization (where the alien usually had a minimum of three to five years of legal permanent residence and was seeking to become a citizen). The twin emphases on plenary power, on the one hand, and the constitutional significance of an alien's growing stake in society, on the other, could of course controvert one another. Not surprisingly, the Court's jurisprudence in the 1950s was contradictory and confusing. Furthermore, in many respects—notwithstanding *Johnson v. Eisentrager*—the Court's positions in the 1950s marked a retreat from its relatively more liberal positions of the 1940s.

The Court proved especially willing to raise the procedural and substantive bar when the government tried to denaturalize individuals: to set aside a lawful naturalization. This took the form of imposing evidentiary requirements and reading statutes against the grain. In the 1930s, 1940s, and 1950s, apart from the brief period of the U.S.-Soviet wartime alliance, current and former Communist Party members who were naturalized citizens were highly vulnerable to having their citizenship set aside, often because membership in the Communist Party was deemed proof that an individual was not "attached to the principles of the Constitution of the United States," a requirement of naturalization law. Individuals who were member of the Communist Party at the time they naturalized could therefore be accused of having procured naturalization fraudulently, which then became a basis for setting aside the naturalization. In *Schneiderman v. United States* (1943), handed down during the U.S.-Soviet wartime alliance, the Court emphasized the gravity of denaturalization. In stripping an individual of citizenship, the government took away "the priceless benefits that derive from that status." In such an instance, the evidence had to be "clear, unequivocal, and convincing," not the preponderance standard applicable to ordinary civil actions. In the case of the petitioner, the Court embarked on a detailed examination of various tenets of Communist thought before concluding that "where two interpretations of an organization's program are possible, the one reprehensible and a bar to naturalization and the other permissible, a court in a denaturalization proceeding ... is not justified in canceling a certificate of citizenship ... ." Were the law otherwise, the Court cautioned, "valuable rights would rest upon a slender reed, and the security of the status of our naturalized citizens might depend in considerable degree upon the political temper of the times."[96]

But as the U.S.-Soviet alliance splintered, and paranoia about Communism in the early 1950s mounted, the Court retreated from the high procedural and substantive barriers it had erected against the government's ability to strip citizenship from naturalized citizens. The constitutional weight accorded an immigrant's stake in American society, laid out in *Johnson v. Eisentrager*, fell away as plenary power was reaffirmed in the context of deporting Communists. An argument can of course be made that the Court's different positions on denaturalization (strong protection) and deportation (affirmation of plenary power) was consistent with *Johnson v. Eisentrager*: after all, naturalized citizens presumably have a greater stake in American society than do long-term permanent residents. But the Court's increasing harshness from the 1940s to the 1950s can be seen also in the changing treatment it meted out to long-term permanent residents subject to deportation.

In the 1940s, the Court remained relatively protective of the constitutional freedoms of resident aliens. In *Kessler v. Strecker* (1939), the Court ruled that resident aliens who had once been members of the Communist Party but had terminated their membership prior to arrest could not be subject to deportation.[97] Congress responded by passing the Alien Registration Act of 1940, which provided for the deportation of aliens who had been members of a subversive group "at any time."[98] In a celebrated concurrence in *Bridges v. Wixon* (1945)—a case argued during the U.S.-Soviet alliance in which the Court quashed the deportation order against Communist labor organizer Harry Bridges—Justice Murphy reasoned thus: "Since resident aliens have constitutional rights, it follows that Congress may not ignore them in the exercise of its 'plenary' power of deportation. ... The First Amendment and other portions of the Bill of Rights make no exception in favor of deportation laws or laws enacted pursuant to a 'plenary' power of government."[99]

But as the Cold War intensified in the 1950s, the Court showed increasing deference to the government's efforts to deport former Communists, even when the immigrant's stake in American society might have warranted judicial intervention on the immigrant's behalf. In *Harisiades v. Shaughnessy* (1952), and then again in *Galvan v. Press* (1954), the Court approved the deportation of former members of the Communist Party, each of whom had been a legal permanent resident for over three decades, under deportation statutes that were enacted *after* their membership had ceased. In other words, membership in the Communist Party had not been grounds for deportation when they were members. Nevertheless, the Court approved the deportations in the name of plenary power, finding no violation of the Due Process Clause, the *Ex Post Facto* Clause, or the First Amendment.[100] Seemingly in recognition of the harshness of this position, the Court softened the blow by signaling that it would read deportation statutes narrowly.[101]

During the 1950s, the Court also adopted harsh positions when it came to according aliens procedural protections (protections that had long been a way of softening the impact of plenary power). Indeed, the Court's pronouncements on the procedural protections due aliens subject to exclusion were, hard as it might be to conceive, almost harsher than they had been at the height of the Chinese exclusion era. *United States ex. rel. Knauff v. Shaughnessy* (1950) involved an alien seeking admission as a war bride who was excluded and denied an admission hearing before a board of inquiry on the ground that her exclusion was based on confidential security information. The Court refused to find a constitutional problem. Exclusion was a part of Congress' sovereign right and the Constitution did not require that it provide any procedural protections. As the Court put it: "Whatever the procedure authorized by Congress is, it is due process as far as an alien denied entry is concerned."[102]

An even harsher rule was applied to the case of a returning resident alien, who found himself excluded when he tried to return home to the United States. In the dramatic case of Ignatz Mezei—who had lived in the United States from 1923 to 1948, but then left the United States for eighteen months to visit his dying mother in Rumania—the Court reaffirmed its ruling in *Knauff*, treating Mezei no differently from an alien seeking admission for the first time, notwithstanding his quarter century of continuous residence. Worse still Mezei was subjected to indefinite exclusion in New York harbor: the United States would not admit him and no other country would take him back. The Court's conclusion was unequivocal: "[W]e do not think that respondent's continued exclusion deprives him of any statutory or constitutional right."[103]

In a companion case decided that same year, however, the Court decided to blur the distinction between the exclusion of returning aliens and the deportation of resident aliens. According to a constitutional position going back to the case of *Yamataya v. Fisher* (1903), procedural protections afforded aliens in deportation cases were usually greater than those afforded aliens in exclusion proceedings. In *Kwong Hai Chew v. Colding* (1953), the Court recognized that "if an alien is a lawful permanent resident of the United States and remains physically there, he is a person within the protection of the Fifth Amendment." Such an alien was entitled to Due Process. What was the case, however, if he left the United States only to become the subject of exclusion proceedings on his return? The Court ruled that his constitutional status was not terminated by the mere fortuity of having left the country: "[f]rom a constitutional point of view, he is entitled to due process without regard to whether or not, for immigration purposes, he is to be treated as an entrant alien ... ."[104]

So how was one to reconcile *Mezei* with *Kwong Hai Chu*? The constitutional difference between them rested, apparently, on the comparative length of the alien's absence from the United States: a month or two (*Kwong Hai Chu*) versus eighteen months (*Mezei*). However, by the light of the *Johnson v. Eisentrager* view that aliens' protections be increased commensurately with their stake with American society, the decisions were harder to reconcile: in *Kwong Hai Chu*, a permanent resident for approximately five years was treated as an insider; in *Mezei*, an alien who had been a permanent resident for twenty-five years was treated as a rank outsider. Even as it recognized the importance of the immigrant's stake in American society, in other words, the 1950s Court sometimes failed to accord it proper weight.

The 1960s marks the high noon of the civil rights era and a period of great change in American immigration law. The Hart-Celler Act of 1965 should be seen as part of the larger transformation in federal law that included the passage of the Civil Rights Act of 1964 and the Voting Rights Act of 1965. For the first time in American history, a worldwide legal immigration system came into being; the highly unequal quota structure of earlier immigration laws came to an end. Immigration into the United States would take place under two broad heads: family ties and labor. This does not mean, however, that the Hart-Celler Act was not restrictionist. It created stricter controls over labor migration than had hitherto existed and limited the power of the president to provide special refugee admissions. Most important, it placed admissions from the Western Hemisphere under numerical restrictions for the first time: 170,000 slots were allotted to countries in the Eastern Hemisphere (with country quotas, albeit equal ones) and 120,000 were reserved for countries in the Western Hemisphere (without country quotas). By 1978, new legislation established the same per-country ceilings for both hemispheres: in other words, the traditional preference given to Western Hemisphere countries, long a source of "back door" agricultural labor, was removed.[105]

At the same time, however, there was what could be read as a reinstatement of the older racial preferences of immigration law. Congress had not anticipated, in the Hart-Celler Act, that those immigrating on the basis of family ties or labor (the new preferred bases of immigration) would use up all available quota numbers. With the surge in immigration from the Third World (especially Asia and Latin America), this is precisely what happened. Nonpreference immigration (immigrants without family ties or requisite labor skills), especially from Europe, was crowded out by preference immigration from the Third World. There were complaints that Irish immigrants, in particular, faced reduced immigration opportunities. After trying various formulas, Congress settled on a permanent diversity lottery system, available only to those immigrants from "underrepresented" countries and regions (the system was envisaged to encourage immigration from, and hence was initially tilted towards, Europe; it is now tilted towards Europe and Africa). Since the early 1990s, Congress has divided immigrants into three broad groups: family-based immigrants; employment-based immigrants; and so-called "diversity" immigrants.[106]

The introduction of quotas for immigrants from the Western Hemisphere, combined with the ending of the *bracero* program set up with Mexico in the 1940s, established the conditions under which illegal immigration, especially from Mexico, worsened. The problem of illegal immigration from Mexico and Central America became, in turn, a major focus of immigration law from the 1970s on. In 1986, Congress passed the Immigration Reform and Control Act (IRCA), an attempt to mitigate the problem of illegal immigration by offering illegal aliens the opportunity to legalize their status and by imposing sanctions on U.S. employers. As a consequence of the law, all-time highs of 1.5 million and 1.8 million immigrants were officially admitted to permanent residence in 1990 and 1991.[107]

By the mid-1990s, even as there was willingness on the part of policymakers to open the door to highly skilled and propertied immigrants, Congress and the country as a whole were once again swept up by an anti-immigrant mood, focused this time on undocumented immigrants who had been convicted of crimes and who sought welfare. The result was three statutes, all passed in 1996: the Antiterrorism and Effective Death Penalty Act, the Illegal Immigration Reform and Immigrant Responsibility Act, and the Personal Responsibility and Work Opportunity Reconciliation Act (the last was the general welfare reform statute). Together, these statutes streamlined and accelerated the removal of noncitizens with criminal records; restricted judicial review of administrative removal orders with respect to immigrants deportable because of their criminal backgrounds; and restricted immigrant access to most means-tested benefit programs. Since 2001, a major focus of immigration law has also been terrorism. The USA Patriot Act (2001) and the Enhanced Border Security and Visa Entry Reform Act (2002) expanded the definition of "terrorist" for purposes of exclusion and deportation and tightened requirements for obtaining a visa to enter the United States.[108]

Not surprisingly, the number of formal removals shot up dramatically after 1996, leading scholars such as Daniel Kanstroom to label the contemporary United States a "deportation nation."[109] In the fiscal year 1990, there were 30,000 noncitizens deported. By contrast, in fiscal year 2005, nearly 210,000 noncitizens were deported, the bulk of them to Latin America and the Caribbean. Immigrants from such regions, and their families, are the internal foreigners of today. Latino and Caribbean families, composed of immigrants and citizens, are disproportionately represented among the undocumented, disproportionately likely to suffer exploitative labor conditions, disproportionately likely to experience disruptions as a result of deportation, and, relative to other immigrants, more likely to suffer from the withdrawal of benefits.

Today's deportation traffic presents special paradoxes that critics have been quick to point out. To be sure, those deported are not citizens of the United States: they are, in a formal sense, outsiders. But many came to the U.S. as children, grew up and acquired their identities and habits here, and know no other country. They are, effectively, insiders but for the fortuity of never having naturalized. A 1997 *New York Times* article stated the problem as follows.

> American gang habits—and the branches of the gangs themselves—are being exported to El Salvador and other countries in and around the Caribbean. In these smaller cultures, weak police forces already have their hands full struggling to control individual crimes or politically motivated violence. Now the police face slick, organized, well-armed gangs that operate with all the truculence of their parent groups in Los Angeles and other American cities. ...
>
> Throughout [El Salvador], thousands of young men, recruited and led by deportees who learned their trade on the streets of American cities, have been joining the gangs, which officials blame for much of a marked postwar increase in violence and criminality. ...
>
> The gangs bring with them a deadly rivalry that dates to their founding in Los Angeles. And when not trying to kill each other, their members rob travelers, rape women, steal cars, deal in drugs and extort businesses.

> Since 1993, more than 4,000 Salvadorans, mostly teen-agers and young adults with United States criminal records have been forcibly repatriated to a homeland that many of them barely remembered, since most were children when they fled this country as refugees during the civil war. ...
>
> Even after they are returned to the countries of their births, officials throughout the region note, deportees maintain ties to the gangs to which they belonged in the United States and continue to cooperate with them in criminal activities. Here, for instance, gang members are reported by the police to receive and resell cars stolen by former comrades in California and Texas and to be involved in illegally transporting would-be immigrants to the United States.[110]

Such accounts suggest that the current drive on the part of the U.S. government to deport criminal aliens commits an injustice with respect to the societies compelled to accommodate what might justly be called American social problems by virtue of certain American criminals' lack of American citizenship.[111] They also underscore the profound hardships suffered by citizens and noncitizens alike when individuals with very little connection to their countries of birth are returned there after decades of residence in the United States.

From a constitutional perspective, the liberalization of immigration law after 1965 did not mean that the plenary power doctrine crumbled. Indeed, it was affirmed in the exclusion, deportation, and naturalization contexts and continues to undergird the torrent of deportations today. Plenary power in such contexts, in turn, was invoked to justify the federal government's discrimination between citizens and aliens in the welfare rights context. In *Mathews v. Diaz* (1976), the Court explicitly grounded the constitutional permissibility of Congress' decision to deny immigrants welfare benefits in its plenary power over immigration and naturalization.

> In the exercise of its broad power over naturalization and immigration, Congress regularly makes rules that would be unacceptable if applied to citizens. The exclusion of aliens and the reservation of the power to deport have no permissible counterpart in the Federal Government's power to regulate the conduct of its own citizenry. The fact that an Act of Congress treats aliens differently from citizens does not in itself imply that such disparate treatment is 'invidious.'[112]

Nevertheless, in decisions affirming federal plenary power, the impact of the broader civil rights revolution registered in the energetic dissents of certain members of the Court (notably, Justice Thurgood Marshall) who recognized that decisions with respect to aliens were inevitably decisions with respect to citizens: that it was impossible to separate outsiders from insiders. Two of the leading post-1965 plenary power cases are discussed below.

According to the facts in *Kleindienst v. Mandel* (1972), Ernest Mandel, a well-known Belgian Marxist scholar, was excludable under provisions of the pre-1990 Immigration and Nationality Act, which barred "anarchists," "those who advocate or teach ... opposition to all organized government," and members of any branch of the Communist Party. In 1969, Mandel applied for a nonimmigrant visa to attend conferences in the United States and was denied admission. Mandel and those who had invited him filed suit. The Court dismissed the argument that Mandel's exclusion infringed upon the First Amendment rights of his American hosts and therefore should be set aside. Although First Amendment rights might be implicated, the Court refused to budge from the line of cases setting forth the plenary power doctrine: "Over no conceivable subject is the legislative power of Congress more complete than it is over [the admission of aliens]." Therefore, when the executive (as a result of delegation by Congress) "exercises this power negatively on the basis of a facially legitimate and bona fide reason, the courts will neither look behind the exercise of that discretion, nor test it by balancing its justification against the First Amendment interests of those who seek personal communication." Justice Douglas' dissent explicitly compared *Kleindienst* with the *Chinese Exclusion Case*: "An ideological test, not a racial one, is used here. But neither, in my view, is permissible ... ." Justice Thurgood Marshall's dissent—adopting a position similar to the one he would adopt in *Fiallo v. Bell* (discussed below)—emphasized that U.S. citizens' rights were at stake. He would have applied current First Amendment jurisprudence to the facts at hand and extended the Bill of Rights to the federal government's exclusion power.[113]

In the context of admission to permanent residence, the Court also reaffirmed the plenary power doctrine. In *Fiallo v. Bell* (1977), individuals challenged a provision of the Immigration and Nationality Act that defined the word "child" to exclude illegitimate children of natural fathers, but not illegitimate children of natural mothers. The result was that, under the law, illegitimate children of natural fathers could neither be sponsored as immigrants, nor sponsor their natural fathers as immigrants. Were this law to have existed in a domestic context, it would likely have been struck down; because it related to immigrants, however, it was sustained. Declaring that "the reasons that preclude judicial review of political questions also dictate a narrow standard of review of decisions ... in the area of immigration and naturalization," the Court upheld the law. In fact, the Court, declared that "[i]t is not the judicial role in cases of this sort to probe and test the justifications for the legislative decision."

Justice Marshall registered a vigorous dissent in *Fiallo*, arguing that the law applied unequally with respect to different classes of American citizens. As he put it:

> It is irrelevant that aliens have no constitutional right to immigrate and Americans have no constitutional right to compel the admission of their families. The essential fact is that Congress did choose to extend such privileges to American citizens but then denied them to a small class of citizens. When Congress draws such lines among citizens, the Constitution requires that the decision comport with Fifth Amendment principles of equal protection and due process. The simple fact that discrimination is set in immigration legislation cannot insulate from scrutiny the invidious abridgement of citizens' fundamental interests.

As with his dissent in *Kleindienst v. Mandel*, Justice Marshall would have subjected immigration law to the broader changes in constitutional law—in this case, to the Court's gender-equality jurisprudence. Denouncing "discrimination [that] would be intolerable in any context but immigration," he accused the majority of "condon[ing] the invidious discrimination in this case simply because it is embedded in the immigration laws ... ."[114]

In the face of such energetic dissents, in recent years, even in decisions affirming the federal government's actions, the Court has taken to providing hints that substantive provisions of the Constitution might end up limiting plenary power. *Fiallo v. Bell* is good example. Even as the Court in the case affirmed Congress' plenary power over exclusion, it buried in a footnote the suggestion that "[o]ur cases reflect acceptance of a limited judicial responsibility under the Constitution even with respect to the power of Congress to regulate the admission and exclusion of aliens ... ."[115] More recently, the Court has attempted to establish a relationship between citizenship law and equal protection jurisprudence. The question has arisen in the context of citizenship *jure sanguinis*, or citizenship transmitted through blood, rather than citizenship *jure soli*. If Congress had removed the most egregious forms of gender discrimination against women in citizenship law by the 1930s, forms of discrimination between men and women remained, some in ways that disadvantaged men. Section 309 of the Immigration and Nationality Act made it more difficult for citizen fathers to transmit citizenship *jure sanguinis* to children born outside the United States out of wedlock than it did for citizen mothers. Specifically, there were additional onerous requirements of proof of paternity. In *Miller v. Albright* (1998), the government argued for "deference to congressional decisions concerning immigration and naturalization" on the ground that "policies toward the admission to this country, and most especially to full citizenship therein, of those not born here are uniquely political in character, dealing as they do with the threshold question of who is entitled to any share in the benefits, protections, and responsibilities of the democratic compact that the Constitution represents."[116] When the Court considered the constitutionality of the same law in *Nguyen v. INS* (2001), it did not reach the government's plenary power argument because it found that the law met the constitutional standard applied to gender based discrimination.[117] At least implicitly, therefore, the Court's Equal Protection jurisprudence might be seen to be applicable to citizenship law.[118]

The post-1965 Court has proved more willing to accord procedural protections based on differing kinds of "stake" than did the Court of the 1950s. Breaking with the 1953 *Mezei* case in *Landon v. Plasencia* (1982), the Court affirmed the right to due process for returning permanent resident aliens facing exclusion hearings.[119] Because of the increased gravity of the deprivation, deportation proceedings have to afford greater procedural protections than do exclusion proceedings.[120] After the 1996 immigration reforms—and as Congress cut back on judicial review in cases involving immigrants deportable by reason of having committed particular classes of crimes—the Court sought actively to preserve immigrants' procedural safeguards.[121] More recently, in *Zadvydas v. Davis* (2001)—a major decision handed down only weeks before the September 11 attacks that departs as well from the Cold War *Mezei* case—the Court has said that aliens subject to deportation may not be held indefinitely if there is no reasonable likelihood that their deportation will be accomplished.[122] In the post 9/11 period, both the government and the courts have invoked the plenary power doctrine to justify the selective detention of noncitizens of particular backgrounds.[123]

Perhaps the greatest development of the post-World War II era, however, has been the Court's wielding of preemption and equal protection theories to strike down state laws discriminating between citizens and aliens. Federal plenary power has been affirmed, thereby increasing the difference between citizen and alien; and yet, in striking down state alienage laws, the Court has simultaneously undermined the difference between citizen and alien.[124]

Beginning in the mid-twentieth century, the Court began to alter its early twentieth-century alienage jurisprudence, becoming far more aggressive in applying equal protection notions to state statutes and scaling back its "special public interest" doctrine. In *Takahashi v. Fish & Game Commission* (1948), the Court struck down a 1943 California statute that barred the issuance of a commercial fishing license to any "alien Japanese" (later amended to bar any "person ineligible to citizenship"). The Court rejected California's argument that the state was the owner-trustee of all fish in its coastal waters. At the same time, it recognized that California was engaged in race-based discrimination:

"It does not follow, as California seems to argue, that because the United States regulates immigration and naturalization in part on the basis of race and color classifications, a state can adopt one or more of the same classifications to prevent lawfully admitted aliens within its borders from earning a living in the same way that other state inhabitants earn their living."[125] Soon thereafter, the Court also struck down the alien land laws that had been instituted in the early twentieth century.[126] Various professions once closed to aliens were opened up in the second half of the twentieth century.

However, in the 1970s and 1980s, the Court went much further, preventing state discrimination against aliens in the important area of welfare rights. In *Graham v. Richardson* (1971), the Court struck down Arizona and Pennsylvania welfare statutes that made citizenship a prerequisite to receiving state welfare. In these cases, the Court openly asserted its post-New Deal role as protector of minorities. Aliens constituted a "discrete and insular minority" within the meaning of *United States v. Carolene Products*, maintained the Court, and therefore alienage classifications were, under the Equal Protection Clause, "inherently suspect and subject to close judicial scrutiny."[127] This was the first time that alienage was added to the list of constitutionally "suspect" classifications under the Equal Protection Clause. Various reasons—changes in the "special public interest doctrine," the collapse of the right-privilege distinction, and the newly recognized constitutional right to travel—undergirded the Court's equal protection arguments in these cases. Furthermore, the Court reasoned, the state welfare statutes constituted interferences with the federal government's exclusive power over immigration.[128]

In *Plyler v. Doe* (1982), the Court went further still, holding that the Equal Protection Clause prohibited Texas from denying public education to the foreign-born children of undocumented aliens. The decision was more controversial than *Graham v. Richardson* because the Court could not rely unambiguously on preemption theories. Congress had expressed a strong policy of dissuading undocumented immigration, and Texas' law, if anything, bolstered this effort. Nevertheless, according to Justice Brennan, Texas' law "could hardly be considered rational" in the absence of "some substantial goal of the State"; in his opinion, the state had demonstrated no such "substantial goal."[129] The law was troubling, according to the Court, because it "raise[d] the specter of a permanent caste of undocumented resident aliens, encouraged by some to remain here as a source of cheap labor, but nevertheless denied the benefits that our society makes available to citizens and lawful residents. The existence of such an underclass presents most difficult problems for a Nation that prides itself on adherence to principles of equality under law." *Plyler v. Doe* was a major victor for

MALDEF, the Mexican American Legal Defense and Education Fund. It played a significant role in public debates over undocumented immigration during the 1980s and undoubtedly strengthened calls for what became an eventual 1986 "amnesty" for undocumented aliens.

Since then, a combination of equal protection and preemption doctrines have resulted in the invalidation of various state-level initiatives to police or withhold benefits from undocumented aliens.[130] This has not, of course, prevented border and other states, swept up in anti-immigration fervor, from attempting to regulate benefits to immigrants and to step up state enforcement of immigration laws. Such attempts such as the most recent attempt in Arizona have often been ruled unconstitutional.[131]

But if the Court went far in striking down state discrimination on the ground of alienage, by the 1980s there was also distinct scaling back. In *Cabell v. Chavez-Salido* (1982), the Court considered a California law that made citizenship a prerequisite for employment as a state "peace officer," and declared an end to the era of the "special public interest" doctrine used to such great effect in the early twentieth century. But this did not mean that all state discrimination on the basis of alienage was now impermissible. The Court now distinguished between the economic and sovereign functions of government. *Graham v. Richardson* had determined that citizenship was not relevant grounds for a state's denial of economic benefits. However, citizenship remained a permissible basis of state discrimination when it came to certain kinds of sovereign functions. The Court put it thus:

> The exclusion of aliens from basic governmental processes is not a deficiency in the democratic system but a necessary consequence of the community's process of political self-definition. Self-government, whether direct or through representatives, begins by defining the scope of the community of the governed and thus of the governors as well: Aliens are by definition outside of this community. Judicial incursions in this area may interfere with those aspects of democratic self-government that are most essential to it.

Accordingly, the Court applied a two-pronged constitutional test: examining the specificity of the classification and whether the classification applied to "persons holding state elective or important nonelective executive, legislative, and judicial positions," those officers who "participate directly in the formulation, execution, or review of broad public policy" and hence "perform functions that go to the heart of representative government." The Court found that California "peace officers" met the requirements of this test.[132]

In the early twenty-first century, then, constitutional law in the contexts of immigration and citizenship might be characterized as follows: a strong affirmation of federal plenary power in the context of exclusion, deportation, naturalization, and welfare rights, albeit with some hints that substantive provisions of the Constitution might limit federal plenary power; an insistence on procedural rights for resident aliens in exclusion and deportation proceedings; and an aggressive wielding of equal protection and preemption doctrines to counter state laws discriminating against aliens. The constitutional law of immigration and citizenship has long allowed the federal government to draw strong lines separating insiders from outsiders, but has then undermined that position by mandating a measure of parity in the realms of procedure and, especially, at the level of state alienage laws.

Conclusion

The United States has been more receptive to immigrants than has the rest of the world. But the country's celebration of itself as a nation of immigrants committed to abstract values should not blind us to the exclusions, biases, and prejudices that have afflicted—and that continue to afflict—the American immigration and citizenship order.

The Court can lay claim to a mixed historical record: sometimes sanctioning the perpetration of exclusions, biases, and prejudices vis-à-vis immigrants; sometimes protecting the immigrant population from them. Insofar as the Court has upheld federal plenary power and state-level alienage laws from the late nineteenth century onwards, it has endorsed the worst excesses of American anti-immigrant sentiment, ideological paranoia, and racial and ethnic prejudice. The Court's role before the invention of federal plenary power has been even less admirable. Prior to the Civil War, the Court played an active role in defending slavery and enforcing blacks' lack of citizenship, all of which had the effect of keeping immigration restrictions stuck at the state level. In other words, the Court played an integral role in allowing government to separate citizen from alien in draconian ways along various troubling axes.

But even as the Court has upheld the worst excesses of federal and state power, it has also—perhaps in recognition of its position—sought to undermine governmental excesses in all kinds of ways. It has recently hinted that substantive provisions of the Constitution might limit federal plenary power; it has long emphasized growing levels of procedural protection owing to immigrants as their stake in American society increases (even if it has not always lived up to this idea); and it has applied equal protection and preemption jurisprudence vis-à-vis state laws discriminating against immigrants. It has thereby challenged the differences between citizen and alien, insider and outsider, as legislatures have configured them.

One should not exaggerate the force of this countervailing tendency: it has not always shielded immigrants and their advocates from the overwhelming power of the state. Constitutional law in this area remains heavily tilted in the direction of governmental power, and the government continues to rely on this constitutional structure to come down hard on immigrants (as, for example, in the massive post-1996 expansion of deportation). Nevertheless, the willingness of courts occasionally to recognize outsiders as insiders has allowed immigrants and their advocates to create spaces of opportunity. If the law insists on setting insiders apart from outsiders, but then also on undermining the difference between insiders and outsiders, immigrants and their advocates can engage in their own scrambling and unscrambling in order to challenge the state. It is in such struggles between the state and immigrants—struggles that have mostly but not always tilted in favor of the state—that the history of immigration and citizenship law inheres. Wherever the current state of the law lies, its long history, with its many twists and turns, suggests the law's constructedness and the possibility that it can always be rethought, re-fought, and remade.

Further Reading

Those interested in the history of how the U.S. Constitution has related to questions of immigration and citizenship will be able to cast a very wide net indeed. In recent years, scholars across a range of disciplines (law, history, sociology, and political science) have devoted considerable attention to the legal history of immigration and citizenship.

Modern scholarship draws our attention repeatedly to the profoundly inegalitarian ways in which U.S. citizenship was extended among the native-born population in the late eighteenth and early nineteenth centuries. James Kettner's classic *The Development of American Citizenship* (1978) offers a penetrating account of the seventeenth century English ideas that informed American citizenship, dwells at length on late eighteenth- and early nineteenth-century debates about voluntary allegiance, and then traces the tortured development of U.S. citizenship up to the *Dred Scott* decision in 1857. A recent addition to the literature on eighteenth-century citizenship, Douglas Bradburn's *The Citizenship Revolution: Politics and the Creation of the American Union, 1774–1804* (2009), adds fascinating details not covered by Kettner. Rogers Smith's monumental *Civic Ideals* (1997) covers a larger terrain. It emphasizes the twinning of liberalism and ascriptive inegalitarianism in the unfolding of American citizenship over the course of the long nineteenth century. Barbara Welke's compact *Law and the Borders of Belonging in the Long Nineteenth Century United States* (2010), dealing with the same period, underscores how law across the nineteenth century withheld citizenship and personhood on axes of race, gender, sexuality, and disability. The authoritative work on the racialization of citizenship in the post-1870s naturalization context is Ian Haney Lopez' *White by Law* (1996). The work of Linda Kerber, Nancy Cott, Candice Bredbenner, and Martha Gardner traces the deeply gendered and racialized nature of citizenship.[133]

Modern scholarship on the history of immigration restriction has kept pace with the literature on citizenship. Historians have moved past the older frameworks of immigration history—best exemplified by Oscar Handlin's *The Uprooted* (1952)—to focus increasingly on the productive role of law in shaping immigration flows. To be sure, earlier works such as John Higham's *Strangers in the Land* (1955) have influenced newer histories of immigration restriction.[134]

Historians had long been aware of state-level immigration regimes in the antebellum period.[135] However, Gerald Neuman's important and exhaustively researched article, "The Lost Century of American Immigration Law" (1993), was the first in recent years to draw scholarly attention to the plethora of regimes of territorial restriction—internal and external—that preceded the national immigration regime.[136] Neuman painstakingly detailed regimes applicable to the poor, the criminal, the sick, and free blacks. In *Strangers to the Constitution* (1996), Neuman expanded on his 1993 essay to discuss a range of legal issues pertinent to antebellum immigration, including the Commerce Clause jurisprudence discussed in this essay.[137] Building upon Neuman's work, Kunal Parker focused upon the experience of antebellum Massachusetts, tracing the shift from a local to a state-level immigration regime between 1780 and 1860 and drawing attention both to the new, and negative, uses of citizenship in antebellum America and to the willful blurring of the distinction between citizen and alien, native and immigrant, when it came to dealing with the poor.[138]

Much of the work on the legal history of immigration has focused the activities of the post-1870 national immigration regime. T. Alexander Aleinikoff's *Semblances of Sovereignty: The Constitution, the State, and American Citizenship* (2002) makes explicit the intimate doctrinal links among plenary power over immigrants, federal authority over Native Americans, and the uneven extension of the U.S. Constitution to territories acquired after the Spanish-American War.[139] A seminal work on the legal history of Chinese exclusion is Lucy Salyer's *Laws Harsh as Tigers* (1995). Focusing on the late nineteenth and early twentieth centuries, Salyer traces how the efforts of Chinese immigrants to use the judicial system provided the impetus for concentrating power in the hands of immigration officials and for the curtailment of judicial review. Salyer offers a brilliant account of immigration as one major site at which to witness of the emergence of the American administrative state. Mae Ngai's *Impossible Subjects: Illegal Aliens and the Making of Modern America* (2004) carries the story forward, offering a complex account of the intertwining of race and nationality in the passage of the quota legislation of the 1920s and then tracing the emergence of the figure of the "illegal alien." Ngai continues with a discussion of the connections between immigration and America's colonial policies, ending with an analysis of post-World War II immigration reform. Kunal Parker's essay "U.S. Citizenship and Immigration Law (1800–1924): Resolutions of Membership and Territory" brings together much of the relevant literature—statutory and constitutional—for the long nineteenth century.[140]

The most recent comprehensive book on immigration policy is political scientist Aristide Zolberg's *A Nation by Design: Immigration Policy in the*

Fashioning of America (2006).¹⁴¹ Zolberg's work is indispensable principally because of its scope: it extends from the American Revolution to today. If not heavily focused on constitutional law, Zolberg is especially strong on canvassing legislative debates in the post-World War II period. A shortcoming of the work: especially for earlier periods, it goes too far in *federalizing* immigration—often through exaggerating the importance of pre-1865 federal legislation or overemphasizing writers on immigration policy—long before immigration in fact became a federal affair. Nevertheless, because of its scope and scale, this is the book to which scholars will be turning for many years to come.

Scholars with legal training and appointments at law schools have carried out comprehensive lawyerly work on the relationships among the U.S. Constitution, citizenship, and immigration. Law review articles written in this area are too numerous to be cited. Because its audience is often legal scholars and practitioners, and its focus contemporary, this scholarship might be inaccessible to scholars trained in the humanities and social sciences with an interest in understanding immigration and citizenship law in a broader historical context. In what follows, I will therefore present only the broadest outlines of this area.[142]

Most scholars of immigration and citizenship law remain highly critical of the plenary power doctrine, seeing in it a sanction for absolute federal power devoid of constitutional restriction. Critiques of the doctrine range from identifying the weakness of the doctrine's grounding in the constitutional text to identifying its imbrication with the racist attitudes of the late nineteenth and early twentieth centuries to bemoaning its incoherence as the Court has tacked this way and that on immigration and citizenship issues to celebrating its limitation in more recent years.[143] It is safe to say that plenary power does not have many defenders in the legal academy. Hiroshi Motomura offers an influential account (one that prefigures the account provided in this essay) of immigration law's tendency to produce—and then undermine through procedural and other surrogates—the distinction between citizen and alien, insider and outsider.[144]

More than anyone else, Linda Bosniak has thoroughly explored the nuances, tensions, and complications of constitutional law's manipulation of the boundary between immigration law and alienage law.[145] Especially as anti-immigrant sentiment has mounted nationally and in border states, many legal scholars have discussed the contemporary intersections of race and ethnicity, immigration, civil rights, and welfare rights.[146] Since 2001, terrorism—and the possibility of selective prosecution of immigrants—has loomed large in immigration debates. David Cole, in particular, has written extensively about the Constitution's application to questions involving terrorist aliens.[147] Following the 1996 immigration law reforms, scholars have taken note of the intersections between immigration law and criminal law; Daniel Kanstroom has drawn attention to the recent drive to deport aliens.[148] For the past decade and a half, legal scholars have also investigated the changing nature of membership and rights, particularly under conditions of globalization.[149]

Notes

1. Thomas Paine, "Common Sense" (1776) in *The Life and Major Writings of Thomas Paine*, ed. Philip S. Foner (New York: Citadel Press, 1945), 31.

2. Herman Melville, *Redburn His First Voyage* (1849; New York: Viking Press, 1983), 185.

3. Emma Lazarus, "The New Colossus," in *Emma Lazarus: Selections from Her Poetry and Prose* (New York: Book League, 1947), 40.

4. Israel Zangwill, "The Melting Pot," in *From the Ghetto to the Melting Pot: Israel Zangwill's Three Jewish Plays*, ed. Edna Nahson (Detroit: Wayne State University Press, 2006).

5. John F. Kennedy, *A Nation of Immigrants* (1958; New York: Harper & Row, 1964).

6. Reed Ueda, *Postwar Immigrant America: A Social History* (Boston: Bedford Books, 1994), 1.

7. For example, in 2009, the United States admitted 1,130,818 immigrants to permanent residence. In 2010, that number was 1,042,625. U.S. Department of Homeland Security, "Yearbook of Immigration Statistics," www.dhs.gov/files/statistics/publications/yearbook.shtm.

8. For example, in 2005, 604,280 immigrants naturalized. U.S. Department of Homeland Security, "2005 Yearbook of Immigration Statistics," http://www.dhs.gov/xlibrary/assets/statistics/yearbook/2005/OIS_2005_Yearbook.pdf.

. Passenger Cases, 48 U.S. (7 How.) 283 (1849), 461 (opinion of Justice Grier).

10. New York v. Miln, 36 U.S. 102, 132 (1837), quoting Vattel, *Law of Nations*, Book 2, Ch. 7, Section 94.

11. Scott v. Sandford, 60 U.S. (19 How.) 393 (1857).

12. Plessy v. Ferguson, 163 U.S. 537 (1896).

13. T. H. Marshall, "Citizenship and Social Class," chap. 4 in *Class, Citizenship, and Social Development* (New York: Doubleday, 1964).

14. For a discussion, see Barbara Y. Welke, *Law and the Borders of Belonging in the Long Nineteenth Century United States* (New York: Cambridge University Press, 2010).

15. Articles of Confederation, Art. IV.

16. James H. Kettner, *The Development of American Citizenship, 1608–1870* (Chapel Hill: University of North Carolina Press, 1978), quoting Madison in *The Federalist*, no. 42.

17. On the impressment controversy, see Roland G. Usher Jr., "Royal Navy Impressment During the American Revolution," *Mississippi Valley Historical Review* 57, no 4 (March 1951): 673–88.

18. Maya Jasanoff, *Liberty's Exiles: American Loyalists in the Revolutionary World* (New York: Alfred A. Knopf, 2011), 6.

19. See Martin v. Massachusetts, 1 Mass. 347, 392 (1805). The case is discussed in Linda K. Kerber, *No Constitutional Right to be Ladies: Women and the Obligations of Citizenship* (New York: Hill and Wang, 1998), 30.

20. U.S. Const. Art. I, Section 2 (citizenship of members of the House of Representatives); Art. I, Section 3 (citizenship of members of the Senate); Art. II, Section 1 (citizenship of President).

21. Act of March 26, 1790 (1 Stat. 103).

22. Act of January 29, 1795 (1 Stat. 414). The aberration was the short-lived Naturalization Act of June 18, 1798 (1 Stat. 566), which increased the naturalization period to fourteen years.

23. "Act for the Better Settlement and Relief of the Poor" (1788, chap. 62), *Laws of the State of New York Passed at the Sessions of the Legislature Held in the Years 1785, 1786, 1787, and 1788, Inclusive* (Albany: Weed Parsons and Company, 1886).

24. "An Act Ascertaining What Shall Constitute a Legal Settlement of any Person in any Town or District Within this Commonwealth," Acts 1793-Chapter 34.

25. U.S. Constitution, Art. I, Section 8.

26. Cherokee Nation v. Georgia, 30 U.S. 1, 16–17 (1831).

27. Johnson v. M'Intosh, 21 U.S. (8 Wheat.) 543 (1823).

28. See generally Vine Deloria Jr. and David E. Wilkins, *Tribes, Treaties and Constitutional Tribulations* (Austin: University of Texas Press, 1999).

29. Massachusetts General Court, House of Representatives, *Free Negroes and Mulattoes* (Boston: True & Green, 1822), 1.

30. See Illinois Constitution of 1848, Article XIV ("The general assembly shall, at its first session under the amended constitution, pass such laws as will effectually prohibit free persons of color from immigrating to and settling in this State; and to effectually prevent the owners of slaves from bringing them into this State, for the purpose of setting them free"); Act of Feb. 12, 1853, Section 3, 1853 Illinois General Laws 354; Indiana Constitution of 1851, Article XIII ("No negro or mulatto shall come into, or settle in, the State, after the adoption of this Constitution"); Act of June 18, 1852, Ch. 74, Section 1, 1852 Ind. Rev. State. 375, 375. See also Act of Feb. 5, 1851, Ch. 72, Section 1, 1850–51 Iowa Acts 172. See generally Gerald L. Neuman, "The Lost Century of American Immigration Law (1776–1875)," *Columbia Law Review* 93, no. 8 (1993): 1833, 1865–80.

31. See Elkison v. Deliesseline, 8 F. Cas. 493 (1823) (Case No. 4,366).

32. See Ira Berlin, *Slaves without Masters: The Free Negro in the Antebellum South* (New York: Pantheon Books, 1974), 372.

33. Moore v. Illinois, 55 U.S. (14 How.) 13, 18 (1853) (Grier, J.).

34. Taney put it thus: "We are all citizens of the United States, and, as members of the same community, must have the right to pass and repass through every part of it without interruption, as freely as in our own States." Passenger Cases (Smith v. Turner; Norris v. Boston), 48 U.S. (7 How.) 283 (1849) 283, 492 (Justice Taney, dissenting).

35. Scott v. Sandford, 60 U.S. (19 How.) 393 (1857).

36. Heirn v. Bridault, 37 Miss. 209, 233 (1859).

37. Mayor of New York v. Miln, 36 U.S. (11 Pet.) 102 (1837).

38. Mayor of New York v. Miln, 147–49. Gibbons v. Ogden, 221 U.S. 1 (1824); Brown v. Maryland, 25 U.S. 419 (1827).

39. Passenger Cases, 428–429 (opinion of Justice Wayne).

40. Passenger Cases, 426 (opinion of Justice Wayne).

41. See Kunal M. Parker, "State, Citizenship, and Territory: The Legal Construction of Immigrants in Antebellum Massachusetts," *Law and History Review* 19, no. 3 (2001): 583, 631.

42. Parker, "State, Citizenship, and Territory," 630–31.

43. U.S. Constitution, Amendment XIV.

44. This did not mean, of course, that blacks or women or other disenfranchised groups thereby became full members of the polity, enjoying the fullest panoply of available rights. In the *Slaughter-house Cases* (1873), the U.S. Supreme Court severely limited the scope of the Fourteenth Amendment's

Privileges and Immunities Clause. In language immediately following the definition of U.S. citizenship, the Fourteenth Amendment provides: "No state shall make or enforce any law which shall abridge the privileges or immunities of citizens of the United States." The Court read this language narrowly, so that "privileges or immunities" in question were linked to the condition of African Americans before the war, and not to any broader conception of citizenship. Slaughter-House Cases, 83 U.S. (16 Wall.) 36 (1873).

45. Elk v. Wilkins, 112 U.S. 94 (1884), 102.

46. The Allotment Act of 1887, also known as the Dawes Act, conferred citizenship on many Indians who resided in the United States. Dawes Act, 24 Stat. 388. Later statutes expanded this grant of citizenship. The Indian Citizenship Act of 1924 gave all Native Americans residing within U.S. territory citizenship. 43 Stat. 253. Since at least 1940, all Native Americans born within the United States are U.S. citizens at birth.

47. Balzac v. Porto Rico, 258 U.S. 298 (1922); Gonzales v. Williams, 192 U.S. 1 (1904); Immigration and Nationality Act, 66 Stat. 235, Section 301(5).

48. Today, *jus soli* rules are in effect in all U.S. territories except American Samoa and Swains Island.

49. Crandall v. Nevada, 73 U.S. (6 Wall.) 35, 41 (1867).

50. Henderson v. Mayor of New York, 92 U.S. 259 (1876); Chy Lung v. Freeman, 92 U.S. 275 (1876).

51. Treaty of July 28, 1868 (16 Stat. 739).

52. Immigration Act of March 3, 1875 (18 Stat. 477).

53. Treaty of November 17, 1880 (22 Stat. 826).

54. Act of May 6, 1882 (22 Stat. 58).

55. Chinese Exclusion Case (Chae Chan Ping v. United States), 130 U.S. 581, 608 (1889).

56. Chinese Exclusion Act of May 5, 1892 (27 Stat. 25).

57. Fong Yue Ting v. United States, 149 U.S. 698, 707 (1893).

58. Act of July 14, 1870 (16 Stat. 254).

59. In re Ah Yup, 5 Sawyer 155, 223 (1878).

60. Lochner v. New York, 198 U.S. 45 (1905). Immigration was only one of the contexts to which plenary power was extended. It is not a little revealing that the federal government's relationship with Native Americans—who were also seen as foreigners (if never accorded the

privileges accorded foreigners)—also came around this time to be governed by plenary power. In *Lone Wolf v. Hitchcock* (1903), the Court held that Congress had plenary power over Indian property and with it the authority to unilaterally abrogate the terms of earlier treaties, provided only that its actions towards its "wards" was guided by "perfect good faith." Lone Wolf v. Hitchcock, 187 U.S. 553 (1903).

61. United States v. Wong Kim Ark, 169 U.S. 649 (1898).

62. Yick Wo v. Hopkins, 118 U.S. 356 (1886); Wong Wing v. United States, 163 U.S. 228 (1896).

63. Immigration Act of March 3, 1891 (26 Stat. 1084).

64. Nishimura Ekiu v. United States, 142 U.S. 651, 660 (1891).

65. The Japanese Immigrant Case (Yamataya v. Fisher), 189 U.S. 86, __ (1903).

66. Immigration Act of August 3, 1882 (22 Stat. 214).

67. Margot Canaday, *The Straight State: Sexuality and Citizenship in Twentieth-Century America* (Princeton: Princeton University Press, 2009), chap. 1.

68. E. P. Hutchinson, *Legislative History of American Immigration Policy, 1798–1965* (Philadelphia: University of Pennsylvania Press, 1981), 414–19.

69. Act of March 3, 1875 (18 Stat. 477); Immigration Act of March 3, 1891 (26 Stat. 1084); Immigration Act of February 20, 1907 (34 Stat. 898).

70. Immigration Act of March 3, 1903, 32 Stat.1213, Section 39.

71. Dillingham Commission Report, vol. 5, *Dictionary of Races or Peoples*, Senate Document 662, Session 61-3 (Washington, DC: Government Printing Office, 1911), 2.

72. Immigration Act of February 5, 1917 (39 Stat. 874).

73. Emergency Quota Act of May 19, 1921 (42 Stat. 5).

74. Immigration Act of 1924 (43 Stat. 153). Filipinos were the only Asians unaffected by the 1924 act. As noncitizen U.S. nationals by virtue of their colonial status, Filipinos were exempt from the law. Their immigration to the United States became restricted in 1934.

75. In re Rodriguez, 81 Fed. 337, 349, 354 (W.D. Texas, 1897).

76. See generally Aristide Zolberg, *A Nation by Design: Immigration Policy in the Fashioning of America* (Cambridge: Harvard University Press, 2006).

77. Act of February 27, 1925 (43 Stat. 1049).

78. Ozawa v. United States, 260 U.S. 178 (1922); Thind v. United States, 261 U.S. 204 (1923). Persons of mixed race could also be excluded. In *In re Young* (1912), a federal court rejected a "half-breed German and Japanese"; and in *In re Alverto* (1912), another federal court excluded an applicant who was one-fourth Spanish and three-fourths Filipino. In re Young, 198 Fed. 715 (W.D. Washington, 1912); In re Alverto, 198 Fed. 688 (E.D. Pennsylvania 1912).

79. Ozawa, 260 U.S. at 197.

80. Thind v. United States, 214.

81. Act of March 2, 1907 (43 Stat. 1228).

82. Mackenzie v. Hare, 239 U.S. 299, 311 (1915).

83. 113 U.S. 27 (1884).

84. Crane v. New York, 239 U.S. 195 (1915); Patsone v. Pennsylvania, 232 U.S. 138 (1914); Clarke v. Deckebach, 274 U.S. 392 (1927). However, the U.S. Supreme Court did strike down an Arizona law that required any employer of more than five employees to employ at least 80 percent qualified electors or native-born citizens of the United States on the ground that it would be inconsistent with the exclusive federal authority to "admit or exclude aliens." Truax v. Raich, 239 U.S. 33 (1915).

85. Terrace v. Thompson, 263 U.S. 197 (1923).

86. U.S. Dept. of Commerce and Labor, Bureau of Immigration, *Treaty, Laws, and Regulations* (1910), 48–53, quoted in Erika Lee, *At America's Gates: Chinese Immigration During the Exclusion Era, 1882–1943* (Chapel Hill: University of North Carolina Press, 2003), 226.

87. Korematsu v. United States, 323 U.S. 214 (1944). See also Roger Daniels, *Concentration Camps: North America* (Malabar, FL: Robert E. Krieger, 1981).

88. 304 U.S. 144 (1938).

89. 314 U.S. 160 (1941).

90. 394 U.S. 618 (1969).

91. Hutchinson, *Legislative History*, 273.

92. Displaced Persons Act of 1948, 62 Stat. 1009; Refugee Relief Act of 1953, 67 Stat. 400, Section 3; War Brides Act of 1945, 59 Stat. 659 Section 1.

93. The ban on homosexual aliens was removed from immigration law in 1990. 1990 Immigration and Nationality Act, 104 Stat. 4978, Section 601. See Barney Frank, "American Immigration Law: A Case Study in the

Effective Use of the Political Process," in *Creating Change: Sexuality, Public Policy, and Civil Rights*, ed. John d'Emilio et al. (New York: St. Martin's Press, 2000), 208–35.

94. 66 Stat. 163, 275.

95. Johnson v. Eisentrager, 339 U.S. 763, 770 (1950).

96. Schneiderman v. United States, 320 U.S. 118, 122, 125, 158 (1943) For the latest, and confusing, test for denaturalization, see Kungys v. United States, 364 U.S. 350 (1960). The judicial solicitude for individuals at risk of denaturalization was also extended to the involuntary expatriation context. Involuntary expatriation differed from denaturalization to the extent that, in the context of the former, there was no defect in an initial naturalization process. In short, involuntary expatriation could be visited upon native-born and naturalized citizens. For many years, the Court's decision in *Mackenzie v. Hare* (1915) governed the question of Congress' extensive powers over the law of expatriation. However, in 1967, in *Afroyim v. Rusk*, the Court ruled that a person could not be involuntarily deprived of U.S. citizenship. The source of authority was the Fourteenth Amendment: "We hold that the Fourteenth Amendment was designed to, and does, protect every citizen of this Nation against a congressional forcible destruction of his citizenship ... ." Afroyim v. Rusk, 387 U.S. 253, 268 (1967). See also Vance v. Terrazas, 444 U.S. 252 (1980).

97. Kessler v. Strecker, 307 U.S. 22 (1939).

98. Alien Registration Act of 1940, Ch. 439, Section 23(b), 54 Stat. 670.

99. Bridges v. Wixon, 326 U.S. 135, 161–62 (1945) (Murphy, J., concurring).

100. Harisiades v. Shaughnessy, 342 U.S. 580, 72 S.Ct. 512 (1952); Galvan v. Press, 347 U.S.522, 74 S.Ct. 737 (1954). Subsequently, the Court cut back on the scope of these rulings, by construing the statutes to require proof of a "meaningful" association with the party before deportation would ensue. See Rowoldt v. Perfetto, 355 U.S. 115, 120 (1957); Gastelum-Quinones v. Kennedy, 374 U.S. 469, 473–78 (1963). Nevertheless, the Court has consistently rejected ex post facto challenges to grounds of deportability. See, e.g.,, Mahler v. Eby, 264 U.S. 32 (1924) (upholding 1920 statute that retroactively applied deportability ground for 1918 conviction under the Selective Draft and the Espionage Acts of 1917); Marcello v. Bonds, 349 U.S. 302, 75 S.Ct. 757 (1955) (upholding 1952 provision that retroactively applied deportability ground or marijuana related offenses to 1938 conviction).

101. Fong Haw Tan v. Phelan, 333 U.S. 6 (1948).

102. United States ex. rel. Knauff v. Shaughnessy, 338 U.S. 537, 544 (1950).

103. Shaughnessy v. United States ex. rel. Mezei, 345 U.S. 206, 215 (1953). Congressional and public pressure eventually secured the release of both Knauff and Mezei.

104. Kwong Hai Chew v. Colding, 344 U.S. 590, 596 (1953).

105. Hart-Celler Act, 79 Stat. 911, Section 201.

106. 1990 Immigration and Nationality act, 104 Stat. 4978. See generally Anna O. Law, "The Diversity Visa Lottery: A Cycle of Unintended Consequences in United States Immigration Policy," *Journal of American Ethnic History* 21, no. 4 (Summer 2002): 3–29.

107. Immigration Reform and Control Act (Simpson-Mazzoli Act), 104 Stat. 3359.

108. U.S.A. Patriot Act, 115 Stat. 272; Enhanced Border Security and Visa Entry Reform Act, 116 Stat. 543.

109. Daniel Kanstroom, *Deportation Nation: Outsiders in American History* (Cambridge: Harvard University Press, 2010).

110. "In U.S. Deportation Policy, a Pandora's Box," *New York Times*, August 10, 1997.

111. See Kunal M. Parker, "Ejecting an Inside: An Essay on the Politics of the Contemporary American Immigration State," in *Critical Beings: Law, Nation and the Global Subject*, ed. Patricia Tuitt and Peter Fitzpatrick (London: Ashgate, 2004).

112. 426 U.S. 67, 94 (1976). *Mathews* was also an important precedent when Congress cut immigrant welfare rights in 1996. City of Chicago v. Shalala, 189 F.3d 598 (7th Cir. 1999), cert. denied, 529 U.S. 1036 (2000). But see Hampton v. Mow Sun Wong, 426 U.S. 88, 96 S.Ct. 1895 (1976).

113. Kleindienst v. Mandel, 408 U.S. 753, 770 (1972) (Douglas, J., dissenting) and 774 (Marshall, J., dissenting).

114. Fiallo v. Bell, 430 U.S. 787, 816 (1977) (Marshall, J., dissenting). In 1986, Congress amended the definition of "child" to cover the relationships at issue in *Fiallo*.

115. Fiallo v. Bell, 430 U.S. 787, 793.

116. Miller v. Albright, 523 U.S. 420, 118 S.Ct. 1428 (1998), brief for the respondent, at 23, 22.

117. Nguyen v. INS, 533 U.S. 53, 121 S.Ct. 2053 (2001).

118. Approximately two decades ago, however, the Ninth Circuit ruled against the government when it tried to deport certain individuals on the ground that their First Amendment rights were involved. Arab-American Anti-Discrimination Committee v. Reno, 70 F.3d 1045 (9th Cir. 1995). On appeal, the Supreme Court ruled for the government on jurisdictional grounds. Reno v. American-Arab Anti-Discrimination Committee, 525 U.S. 471, 119 S.Ct. 936 (1999).

119. Landon v. Plasencia, 459 U.S. 21, 103 S.Ct. 321 (1982).

120. The Court has maintained: "It is well established that the Fifth Amendment entitles aliens to due process of law in deportation proceedings." Reno v. Flores, 507 U.S. 292, 306 (1993). Detention pending removal proceedings has been held to be constitutional. Demore v. Kim, 538 U.S. 510, 123 S.Ct. 1708 (2003).

121. INS v. St.Cyr, 533 U.S. 289 (2001).

122. Zadvydas v. Davis, 533 U.S. 678, 121 S.Ct. 2491 (2001).

123. Arrar v. Ashcroft, F.3d 559 (2d Cir. 2009); al-Marri v. Wright, 487 F.3d 160 (4th Cir. 2007); Al Maqaleh v. Gates, 605 F.3d 94 (D.C. Cir. 2010); Kiyemba v. Obama 555 F.3d 1022 (D.C. Cir. 2009).

124. In general, local governments may not infringe upon the federal government's exclusive immigration power in any way. In the leading preemption case, *De Canas v. Bica* (1976), the Court outlined its preemption doctrine as follows: "Federal regulation should not be deemed preemptive of state regulatory power in the absence of persuasive reasons either that the nature of the regulated subject matter permits no other conclusion, or that the Congress has unmistakably so ordained." In the case involved, California employer-sanctions directed at employers who employed undocumented aliens were deemed not preempted by the Immigration and Nationality Act. De Canas v. Bica, 424 U.S. 351, 96 S.Ct. 933 (1976).

125. Takahashi v. Fish &Game Comm'n, 334 U.S. 410, 418–19, 68 S.Ct. 1138,1142 (1948).

126. Oyama v. California, 332 U.S. 633 (1952).

127. The phrase "discrete and insular minorities" comes from United States v. Carolene Products Co., 304 U.S. 144, 152–53, n.4 (1938).

128. Graham v. Richardson, 403 U.S. 365, 91 S.Ct. 1848 (1971).

129. Plyler v. Doe, 457 U.S. 202, 102 S.Ct. 2382 (1982).

130. See League of United Latin American Citizens v. Wilson, 908 F. Supp. 755 (C.D.Cal. 1995) (invalidating California's Proposition 187).

131. Arizona v. United States, 567 U.S.__ (2012).

132. Cabell v. Chavez-Salido, 454 U.S. 432, 439–441(1982). Ambach v. Norwick, 441 U.S. 68, 99 S.Ct. 1589 (1979); Foley v. Connelie, 435 U.S. 291, 98 S.Ct. 1067 (1978); Sugarman v. Dougall, 413 U.S. 634, 93 S.Ct. 2842 (1973).

133. James H. Kettner, *The Development of American Citizenship, 1608–1870* (Chapel Hill: University of North Carolina Press, 1978); Douglas Bradburn, *The Citizenship Revolution: Politics and the Creation of the American Union, 1774–1804* (Charlottesville: University of Virginia Press, 2009); Rogers M. Smith, *Civic Ideals: Conflicting Visions of Citizenship in U.S. History* (New Haven: Yale University Press, 1997); Barbara Y. Welke, *Law and the Borders of Belonging in the Long Nineteenth Century United States* (New York: Cambridge University Press, 2010); Ian Haney Lopez, *White by Law: The Legal Construction of Race* (New York: New York University Press, 1996); Linda K. Kerber, *No Constitutional Right to be Ladies: Women and the Obligations of Citizenship* (New York: Hill and Wang, 1998); Candice Bredbenner, *A Nationality of Her Own: Women, Marriage, and the Law of Citizenship* (Berkeley: University of California Press, 1998); Nancy Cott, *Public Vows: A History of Marriage and the Nation* (Cambridge: Harvard University Press, 2000); Martha Gardner, *The Qualities of a Citizen: Women, Immigration, and Citizenship, 1870–1965* (Princeton: Princeton University Press, 2005).

134. Oscar Handlin, *The Uprooted: The Story of the Great Migrations That Made the American People* (1952; Philadelphia: University of Pennsylvania Press, 2002); John Higham, *Strangers in the Land: Patterns of American Nativism, 1860–1925* (New Brunswick: Rutgers University Press, 1955).

135. Benjamin J. Klebaner, "State and Local Immigration Regulation in the United States before 1882," *International Review of Social History* 3, no. 2 (1958): 269.

136. Neuman, "The Lost Century of American Immigration Law," 1833.

137. Gerald L. Neuman, *Stranger to the Constitution: Immigrants, Borders, and Fundamental Law* (Princeton: Princeton University Press, 1996). See also Mary Sarah Bilder, "The Struggle over Immigration: Indentured Servants, Slaves and Articles of Commerce," *Missouri Law Review* 61, no. 4 (1996): 743–824.

138. Parker, "State, Citizenship, and Territory," 583. The reader should also consult the vast literature on antebellum nativism directed against Irish and Catholic immigrants. R. A. Billington, *The Protestant Crusade, 1800–1860: A Study of the Origins of American Nativism* (New York: Rinehart

& Co., 1938); Kerby A. Miller, *Emigrants and Exiles: Ireland and the Irish Exodus to North America* (New York: Oxford University Press, 1985).

139. T. Alexander Aleinikoff, *Semblances of Sovereignty: The Constitution, the State, and American Citizenship* (Cambridge: Harvard University Press, 2002). Gerald L. Neuman has also written about the relationship of the U.S. Constitution and territoriality. See the various essays in Neuman, *Strangers to the Constitution*. The most recent and fully developed text on the U.S. Constitution's territorial scope is Kal Raustiala, *Does the Constitution Follow the Flag? The Evolution of Territoriality in American Law* (New York: Oxford University Press, 2009). See also Gary Lawson & Guy Seidman, *The Constitution of Empire: Territorial Expansion and American Legal History* (New Haven, CT: Yale University Press, 2004).

140. Lucy Salyer, *Laws Harsh as Tigers: Chinese Immigrants and the Shaping of Modern Immigration Law* (Chapel Hill: University of North Carolina Press, 1995); Mae Ngai, *Impossible Subjects: Illegal Aliens and the Making of Modern America* (Princeton, NJ.: Princeton University Press, 2004); Kunal M. Parker, "U.S. Citizenship and Immigration Law (1800–1924): Resolutions of Membership and Territory," in *The Cambridge History of Law in America*, ed. Michael Grossberg and Christopher Tomlins (New York: Cambridge University Press, 2008).

141. Aristide R. Zolberg, *A Nation by Design: Immigration Policy in the Fashioning of America* (Cambridge: Harvard University Press, 2006). The reader should also consult other histories of American immigration policies. See, for example, Michael LeMay, *From Dutch Door to Open Door: An Analysis of U.S. Immigration Policy since 1820* (New York: Praeger, 1987); Marion T. Bennett, *American Immigration Policies: A History* (Washington: Public Affairs Press, 1963); Robert A. Divine, *American Immigration Policy, 1924–1952* (New Haven: Yale University Press, 1957). An invaluable guide to immigration legislation is Hutchinson, *Legislative History*.

142. In immigration and citizenship law, as in many other areas, efforts have been made in recent years, however, to tell the "real stories" behind some of the leading immigration and citizenship cases. See David A. Martin and Peter Schuck, eds., *Immigration Stories* (New York: Foundation Press, 2005).

143. For just a few of these critiques, see T. Alexander Aleinikoff, *Semblances of Sovereignty: The Constitution, the State, and American Citizenship* (Cambridge: Harvard University Press, 2002) and "Detaining Plenary Power: The Meaning and Impact of *Zadvydas v. Davis*," *Georgetown Immigration Law Journal* 16 (2002): 365; Louis Henkin, "The Constitution and United States Sovereignty: A Century of Chinese Exclusion and its Progeny," *Harvard Law Review* 100, no. 4 (1987): 853–86.

144. Hiroshi Motomura, "The Curious Evolution of Immigration Law: Procedural Surrogates for Substantive Constitutional Rights," *Columbia Law Review* 92 (1992): 1625.

145. Linda Bosniak, *The Citizen and the Alien: Dilemmas of Contemporary Membership* (Princeton: Princeton University Press, 2006); "Membership, Equality, and the Difference that Alienage Makes," *New York University Law Review* 69 (1994): 1047.

146. David Abraham, "Doing Justice on Two Fronts: The Liberal Dilemma in Immigration" *Ethnic and Racial Studies* 33, no. 6 (2010): 968–85; Linda S. Bosniak, "Opposing Prop. 187: Undocumented Immigrants and the National Imagination," *Connecticut Law Review* 28 (1996): 555; Jennifer Gordon and R. A. Lenhardt, "Citizenship Talk: Bridging the Gap between Immigration and Race Perspectives," *Fordham Law Review* 75 (2007): 2493; Kevin Johnson, "The Case against Racial Profiling in Immigration Enforcement," *Washington University Law Quarterly* 78 (2000): 675; Hiroshi Motomura, "Immigration and Alienage, Federalism and Proposition 187," *Virginia Journal of International Law* 35 (1994): 201; Gerald Neuman, "Aliens as Outlaws: Government Services, Proposition 187, and the Structure of Equal Protection Doctrine," *UCLA Law Review* 42 (1995): 1425. For a critique of state initiatives against immigrants from the federalism perspective, see Michael Wishnie, "Laboratories of Bigotry? Devolution of the Immigration Power, Equal Protection, and Federalism," *New York University Law Review* 76 (2001): 493–569.

147. David Cole and Jules Lobel, *Less Safe, Less Free: Why America is Losing the War on Terror* (New York: New Press, 2007); David Cole, *Enemy Aliens: Double Standards and Constitutional Freedoms in the War on Terrorism* (New York: New Press, 2003); David Cole and Jack Dempsey, *Terrorism and the Constitution: Sacrificing Civil Liberties in the Name of National Security* (New York: New Press, 2002). See also Susan Akram and Kevin Johnson, "Race, Civil Rights, and Immigration after September 11, 2001: The Targeting of Arabs and Muslims," *New York University Annual Survey of American Law* 58 (2002): 295–355; Hiroshi Motomura, "Immigration and We the People after September 11," *Albany Law Review* 66 (2003): 413–29; Gerald L. Neuman, "Terrorism, Selective Deportation and the First Amendment after Reno v. AADC," *Georgetown Law Journal* 14 (2000): 313; Leti Volpp, "The Citizen and the Terrorist," *UCLA Law Review* 49 (2002): 1575.

148. Stephen H. Legomsky, "The New Path of Immigration Law: Asymmetric Incorporation of Criminal Justice Norms," *Washington & Lee Law Review* 64 (2007): 469–528; Juliet Stumpf, "The Crimmigration

Crisis: Immigrants, Crime, and Sovereign Power," *American University Law Review* 56, no. 2 (2006): 367–419; Daniel Kanstroom, *Deportation Nation: Outsiders in American History* (Cambridge: Harvard University Press, 2007).

149. See, for example, T. Alexander and Douglas Klusmeyer, eds., *From Migrants to Citizens: Membership in a Changing World* (Washington, DC: Carnegie Endowment for International Peace, 2000); Linda S. Bosniak, "Citizenship Denationalized," *Indiana Journal of Global Legal Studies* 7 (2000): 447; Peter J. Spiro, *Beyond Citizenship: American Identity after Globalization* (New York: Oxford University Press, 2008).